Publish and Prosper

Intended to help readers succeed in academia by increasing their scholarly productivity, this book provides strategies for getting articles published quickly in reputable research journals. Rather than focusing on the basics of writing about results, this unique guidebook provides tips on how to approach research, maintain motivation, maximize productivity, and overcome common pitfalls so as to become productive scholars. The strategies reviewed will help readers successfully navigate through graduate school, get a good job, receive grants and promotions, and make important contributions to their field.

Written in a breezy style, this book offers case studies, examples, and personal experiences that illustrate the themes of the chapters. Introductions and summaries and key points help to highlight the most critical concepts reviewed in each chapter. Chapter exercises encourage self-reflection and/or the application of the strategies introduced in that chapter. Self-assessment questions in Appendix A help readers pinpoint their strengths and weaknesses. A tracking chart, referred to throughout, provides an effective way to follow the progress of several manuscripts that are at different stages. An interactive version of the chart is available at www.pepstrategies.com along with the time diary and the chapter and self assessment exercises.

Although a young scholar, Nathaniel Lambert has an impressive track record. He already has over 50 papers published in research journals. This book reviews winning strategies practiced by the author and additional insights based on conversations with top producing scholars. By diligently applying this book's core strategies, you too can publish and prosper!

Intended as a reference for students who are planning to attend graduate school and/or pursue an academic career, this book is ideal for professional development and/or research methods courses taught in the behavioral, social, health, and life sciences and for researchers and professionals looking to increase their publication productivity.

Nathaniel M. Lambert is an Assistant Professor of Family Life at Brigham Young University.

Publish and Prosper
A Strategy Guide for Students and Researchers

Nathaniel M. Lambert

NEW YORK AND LONDON

First published 2014
by Routledge
711 Third Avenue, New York, NY 10017

Simultaneously published in the UK
by Routledge
27 Church Road, Hove, East Sussex BN3 2FA

Routledge is an imprint of the Taylor & Francis Group, an informa business

© 2014 Taylor & Francis

The right of Nathaniel M. Lambert to be identified as author of this work has been asserted by him in accordance with sections 77 and 78 of the Copyright, Designs and Patents Act 1988.

All rights reserved. No part of this book may be reprinted or reproduced or utilised in any form or by any electronic, mechanical, or other means, now known or hereafter invented, including photocopying and recording, or in any information storage or retrieval system, without permission in writing from the publishers.

Trademark notice: Product or corporate names may be trademarks or registered trademarks, and are used only for identification and explanation without intent to infringe.

Library of Congress Cataloging-in-Publication Data

A catalog record for this book has been requested.

ISBN: 978-1-84872-993-3 (hbk)
ISBN: 978-1-84872-994-0 (pbk)
ISBN: 978-0-20312-289-1 (ebk)

Typeset in Times New Roman
by Apex CoVantage, LLC

Printed and bound in the United States of America by Walsworth Publishing Company, Marceline, MO.

Contents

List of Figures	vii
Preface	ix
Acknowledgements	xiii
Introduction	xv

PART I
Priorities   **1**

1	Put First Things First	3
2	Choose a Topic That Gets You Out of Bed in the Morning	13
3	See the Vision: Setting Concrete Production Goals That Will Motivate and Inspire You	19
4	Delight in Deadlines and Accountability	25

PART II
Efficiency   **29**

5	Speed Up the Actual Writing Process	31
6	The Snow Fort Principle: Manage Several Ongoing Projects	37
7	Think "Hot Potato": Eliminate Wasted Time	42
8	Find Good Colleagues and Become Everyone's Favorite Collaborator	47

PART III
Pitfall Prevention   **55**

9	Avoid Five Enemies From Within	57
10	Feed the Flame: Avoid Burnout	65

| 11 | Diminish Distractions | 75 |
| 12 | Deal With Rejection | 82 |

PART IV
PEP at Different Career Stages 91

13	Set Up a Productive Graduate Career (Especially for Undergraduates and for Professors Advising Undergraduates)	93
14	From Graduate Student Mentality to Professional Mentality	103
15	The Graduate Student Guide to Be a Great Apprentice, Seek Mentorship, and Become a Mentor	112
16	Transition Into Your First Academic Position	120
17	Mentor Students and Receive Mentorship: A Professor's Guide	126
18	Teach Better in Less Time	132
19	Serve as a Reviewer While Maintaining High Productivity	139
20	Conclusion: Putting It All Together	144

Appendix A: Determining Your Strengths and Weaknesses: A Professional Self-Assessment — 147

Appendix B: Time Diary — 159

Appendix C: Recommended Further Reading — 161

References — 163

Index — 165

Figures

0.1	Principles of Enhanced Productivity	xx
0.2	Principles of Enhanced Productivity	1
1.1	Urgency and Importance Matrix	5
1.2	Research Tasks Represented as Rocks and Other Urgent Tasks are Represented by Sand	7
1.3	The Class Prioritizer	8
1.4	The Research Prioritizer	9
5.1	Principles of Enhanced Productivity	29
9.1	Principles of Enhanced Productivity	55

Preface

What Makes Me Qualified to Write This Book

I once read a book on this topic by someone who hadn't published much himself and I found myself wondering, "How will he teach me how to do something he hasn't done much himself?" Rest assured that although still a young scholar, I have a substantial track record of publications. I published 23 manuscripts before leaving graduate school and 50 manuscripts midway through my second year as a professor. Let me be the first to point out, however, that the success I have experienced is not due to any extraordinarily high level of intelligence. I do consider myself intelligent, but I'm no genius.

When people see my publication record, a common reaction is, "You must never sleep!" I am a hard worker, but I also sleep an average of about 7.5 hours per night and pride myself on having a balanced life. I was able to meet my publication goals without ever working on Sundays and while exercising daily, spending 3–5 hours each day with my family and friends, and pursuing other hobbies such as sports, hiking, and gardening. Thus, although I am indeed a very hard worker, this also is not the secret of my success, considering that many people put in far more hours than I without experiencing the results I have seen.

So if it wasn't superior intelligence or long hours that helped me to discover and apply the keys of publishing success, then what was it? I had not seriously thought about the answer until a friend of mine, knowing of my productive track record while I was in graduate school, said to me, "I simply have no idea how you could possibly have done all that while in graduate school." This comment led to a lot of self-introspection and was actually part of the inspiration behind writing this book.

Essentially, neither high levels of intelligence nor hard work are enough to succeed in becoming a prolific scholar. Rather, I believe the application of core principles and strategies, combined with hard work, is the key to publish and prosper. My objective in writing this book is to clearly communicate these core strategies so you will be able to accomplish more than you've ever thought possible.

What This Book Is Not

My objective in writing this book is to pass along winning strategies, mindsets, and approaches to help you succeed. However, this book is not intended to go over the nuts and bolts of planning, conducting, and writing up research results; plenty of books have been written on such topics. I also assume you will receive training from your mentor, university, or other books to help you with these issues. So rather than being a step-by-step guide to conducting research, this book describes strategies and approaches for the transformative process of becoming a productive scholar.

In addition, although this book is intended for advanced students and new professionals, it is obviously not written in "academese." I use largely informal language and do not support all my points with academic references; in fact, this topic of publishing has surprisingly not been studied much by academics. Rather, the strategies I recommend stem largely from my own experience as well as from my observations and conversations with some of the top producing scholars in my field.

How to Best Use This Book

This book is divided into four parts that detail principles for enhanced productivity, including how to increase the importance and urgency of your research as a key priority (Part I), tips for enhancing your efficiency (Part II), description of productivity pitfalls and how to avoid them (Part III), and how to apply these principles of enhanced productivity at different stages of your career (Part IV). This book is best used as both a guide to give you ideas for improvement and as a workbook of exercises to help you apply what you learn to your professional career. If you are just beginning your research career, you may feel somewhat overwhelmed by all the suggestions; if so, I would suggest implementing the strategies one at a time. You can't expect yourself to go from being a novice researcher to a highly productive scholar overnight, so don't get overwhelmed. Reading this book and then referring to it throughout your career will help you to gradually apply strategies that will enhance your productivity. Remember to move just one step at a time.

Also, your personality style may be different from mine and thus you may find that some strategies appeal to you more than others. For instance, efficiency is a strong value for me, but it may not be such a priority for you. You will likely find several useful tips but not be ready to apply them all at once. Just go at your own pace and implement what you find to be most useful.

I write this book coming from a behavioral and social science background. I have checked it with professor colleagues in other disciplines (e.g., English, history, the humanities, and the hard sciences), and they have told me most of the principles in this book also apply to their fields. However, some of my recommendations may need to be adapted to apply to fields outside the behavioral and social sciences. For instance, scholars who write books do not focus as much on collaboration, but they could apply the principles in the chapter on collaboration for insight to help secure useful feedback from colleagues on their writing and ideas.

I suggest completing the self-assessment questions in the Appendix A first to get a more clear idea of which chapters to focus on the most. Completing the exercises at the conclusion of each chapter will help you get the most out of each chapter. I would also recommend completing the self-assessment questions from Appendix A at the end of every year or school year. This will help provide a sense for which areas you have made improvement in and which areas you still need to work on. All of the chapter exercises and worksheets, the time diary, the manuscript progression chart, and the professional self-assessment included in the book are also available at www.pepstrategies.com for the readers' convenience.

Acknowledgements

I would like to first and foremost acknowledge my wife Olya for being a pillar of strength and support to me through many difficult times. My first undergraduate mentor David Dollahite helped me get my first publications and lit a fire under me regarding the importance of publishing. My graduate advisor Frank Fincham taught me the true purpose of graduate school as well as many of the principles I have included in this book. Alan Hawkins, Steven Graham, Tyler Stillman, Roy Baumeister, and Nathan DeWall gave additional mentorship at key points in my career and I am very grateful for their guidance. I'd like to thank the reviewers commissioned by Routledge: Karen Stamm (University of Rhode Island), Jennifer Rose (Wesleyan University), Tarek Azzam (Claremont Graduate University), and one anonymous reviewer, as well as dozens of colleagues (e.g., Jared Durtschi, Claire Kamp Dush, Paul Silva, Tara Gray), graduate students (e.g., Sesen Negash, Preston Brown, Becky Cobb), and undergraduate students (e.g., Liz Montgomery, Marlea Gwinn) who provided insightful feedback on prior drafts.

Introduction

Main Chapter Points

- Prosperity in academics means you can successfully navigate through graduate school, get a good job, keep your job, and get raises, grants, and other promotions.
- Prosperity also means you garner respect and admiration from others, increase your freedom and flexibility, make important contributions to your field, leave a legacy, and feel intrinsically satisfied.
- You can achieve academic prosperity through priorities, efficiency, and prevention of pitfalls, which can be remembered with the acronym PEP.

My first year of graduate school went terribly, and I seriously wondered if I would ever reach my goal of getting my Ph.D. I felt like my career as an academic had ended before it had really begun. I had achieved a great deal of success in life to this point, and now all I had were shattered dreams and what looked like a very dismal future.

I had to decide right then whether I would let this emotionally debilitating experience determine my fate. I am one who firmly believes you can't control what you are given in life; however, you *can* control how you respond to it. You can either choose to become bitter due to your circumstances or decide to become better. The poet William Ernest Henley once wrote, "I am the master of my fate: I am the captain of my soul." We can either choose to act or to be acted upon. I chose to be the master of my fate; I decided not to give up on my dream of becoming a professor.

I'll never forget the frigid morning in Minnesota as my new advisor and I walked from the conference hotel to grab some breakfast together. I was still a new graduate student and had just presented some research for the first time. It was unusual for a student to present and I was starting to feel good about myself again. My advisor was quick to give me a reality check and told me it was a nice first step, but there was so much more that I needed to do to join the "Big Leagues." He then proceeded to tell me about his most successful graduate student and how much they published together while he was in graduate school. At that moment, I decided I was going to match the productivity level of this preeminent student about whom my advisor always spoke so glowingly, because I wanted to one day be worthy of such praise. I later wrote down my goal of 23 publications by the end of graduate school.

This was a turning point in my career. I now had a clear idea of what I was going to achieve and aligned my priorities toward that goal. I carefully studied successful strategies for increasing research efficiency and how to avoid common pitfalls that prevent people from reaching their goals.

Fast-forward four years through a great deal of hard work and many obstacles along the way. I ended up graduating a year earlier than I'd planned and was still able to reach my goal. I went from wondering if I would ever get my degree, to graduating with distinction; from wondering if I would ever be able to work in the field, to getting my dream job; from moving back and forth from small apartments, to moving into my dream house. My hope now is to help others achieve this kind of success as a way of paying it forward. After all, you are the master of your fate. You can either settle for a career of anxiety and maybe end up perishing, or you can choose to learn what you need in order to have a fulfilling, even prosperous academic career. The choice is yours.

Anxiety and "Perishing" versus Principles for Enhanced Productivity

I imagine you've probably heard the phrase "publish or perish" in reference to professors. This ominous phrase depicts the harsh reality that many professors struggle to publish their work and are consequently dismissed from their position. You may have heard horror stories of professors working so hard that they sleep in their offices for months prior to going up for tenure only to fall short and lose their jobs and sometimes their self-respect. You may know adjunct professors who receive comparatively little pay, few retirement or health benefits, and little job security.

These kinds of stories have most likely left you with a healthy dose of trepidation when thinking about going on the job market or qualifying for tenure. However, it doesn't have to be like this. Although publishing research can be a tricky endeavor and gets more and more competitive with each passing year, you don't have to live in a state of anxiety or in the shadow of the ominously ticking tenure clock. Instead, you can learn to apply key strategies of productivity early on and enjoy the prosperity this will bring you throughout your academic career. In short, you can devote your energy to prospering rather than perishing. I assume you'd like to spend your career prospering. So, what might prospering look like in an academic setting?

The key element of a prosperous academic is being a productive, publishing researcher. You might ask, why is being productive so crucial to my chances of prospering in my academic career? This question is akin to "Why should an artist sell his or her paintings?" or "Why should a doctor see patients?" At a university, publishing is the key form of productivity and is one important way you can make a difference. When you learn how to publish many articles and to publish in good journals, you become prosperous.

So what are the implications of being prosperous? I realize that the word "prosperity" often carries the association of economic well-being. However, the type of prosperity I am referring to is a much broader state of flourishing and thriving. Being prosperous, through using principles for enhanced productivity, means you can successfully navigate through graduate school, get a good job, keep your job through tenure, receive raises and grants, garner respect and admiration from others, increase your freedom and flexibility, make important contributions to your field, leave a legacy, and feel intrinsically satisfied. The next few pages will provide details for each of these that will clearly show the immense benefits of academic prosperity.

Building a Strong Foundation in Graduate School

It is not easy to succeed in graduate school and many don't. In fact, the Council of Graduate Schools reported less than two-thirds of Ph.D. students finish within 10 years (and most of those who don't finish in 10 years will never finish). Additionally, only 49% of humanities Ph.D. students finish in 10 years (Gessner, Jaggars, Rutner, & Tancheva, 2011).

The publishing graduate student is the thriving graduate student. This is the graduate student who has an easy time writing a thesis or a dissertation because this is actually a step down from the rigors of publishing. A productive graduate student will almost always have the good graces of her advisor or department faculty, which is very important for getting a better stipend, scholarships, and connections leading to a job.

Getting a Job

In November of 2010, the National Science Foundation (NSF) reported that 49,562 people earned a Ph.D. in the United States during 2009, the highest number ever recorded. Unfortunately, there are so many people who have a Ph.D. now that many struggle to find any job at all. The NSF report found that only 62.6% of those who completed a Ph.D. in the humanities had any kind of employment at all.

Also, it's getting increasingly difficult to get the coveted tenure-track job. The American Association of University Professors reported that between 1975 and 2009 the number of part-time faculty members has grown by more than 280%! Universities are finding it's much less expensive to hire part-time employees who are not given benefits or a long-term financial commitment. This means there are fewer tenured spots out there, which combined with the oversaturation of people with doctorates, means the competition is extremely fierce. You are judged as a scholar largely based on the publications on your vitae, as many search committees skip right past your cover letter and look at the publication section of your vitae. Although some may argue that they are impeccable teachers, good teaching isn't something that comes across very easily in an application. The only thing that is measurable across all potential scholars is publication record. Rather than being fearful about the usually ominous job application process, imagine being well-prepared and confident and potentially receiving multiple offers you can choose from.

Easily Get Tenure

The phrase "publish or perish" certainly holds its weight when it comes to the tenure process. If you haven't published enough by the end of your 6–7 year window, you perish (you're fired)! Rather than dreading the tenure process as an experience fraught with the anxiety of wondering whether you'll be around next year and what people are saying about you, imagine actually looking forward to the process as an opportunity to showcase your achievements and get a well-deserved raise. My objective is to help you to soar over this tenure hurdle. I want you to be in a position of strength so you will already have made several significant contributions to the literature by the time you go up for tenure. Then there will be little or no question in your mind as to what the outcome will be.

Increase Your Raises and Grant Money

The unproductive faculty members are a drag on the system and aren't rewarded. Most universities reward those who are producing high quantity and high caliber work with better raises. These yearly increases add up substantially over time. In fact, I have a very productive collaborator who started out making around $60,000. He has been significantly rewarded for his productivity and before tenure he was making nearly $75,000 within 5 years. Clearly, raises can be significant for productive scholars. In most disciplines, publishing is a crucial part of getting promoted to full professor.

If grant money is important in your discipline, the skills of conducting and publishing research will transfer very well to writing a grant. Plus, the foundations providing the grant opportunity will be much more inclined to give money to someone who has proved they can publish on the proposed topic. Since most professors don't get paid for a few months of the summer, getting a grant can drastically increase your earning potential as a professor as most grants provide a summer salary.

Respect and Admiration

Publications are the "coin of the realm" and having a lot of those coins will help you gain considerable wealth in the realm of academics, including respect among your colleagues. Publications are the key marker of success in academia and can bring you fame (at least among a relatively small body of researchers in your field) and in some rare cases even fortune (though I wouldn't hold your breath). It is a nice feeling to have people genuinely admire you for your accomplishments.

Freedom and Flexibility

Rather than feeling the pressure to do work you don't really enjoy in order to get something you can publish quickly, imagine having the freedom to pursue whatever interests you. Imagine you have figured out how to be productive to the point that you can stay on top of academic publishing and even write that book you always dreamed of writing on the side. By applying some of the strategies I've included in this book, you can have the freedom to pursue other interests while staying on top of your academic publishing.

Make a Contribution

As you increase in productivity, you can multiply the contributions you can make to knowledge and practice in your field, both by your own work and through the work of your students. It can be thrilling to feel like you are adding to the body of knowledge. As knowledge is increased, the chances are stronger that your work could make a real-world difference to many people. For instance, your research may inform intervention work or therapy and could benefit the lives of many people who are involved. Something you found in a study may help someone live a better life.

Leave a Legacy

Less productive scholars struggle to teach their students something they never learned themselves. As a result, less productive faculty often end up feeling hampered by unproductive students. Instead, picture yourself surrounded by a team of highly producing students that are on their way to becoming leaders in the field. Imagine the important findings that will be cited by future textbooks. What an important legacy you have left! As you learn to be productive yourself, you can pass these strategies on to your students and colleagues and make a positive difference in their careers.

Intrinsic Inner Satisfaction

Many of the indicators of prospering I have mentioned (e.g., raises, tenure, etc.) are more extrinsic in nature. Perhaps one of the most rewarding elements of prospering is the inner feeling of a job well done. Just knowing you have succeeded at one of your primary roles in life will provide you with a great and enduring sense of accomplishment and satisfaction. This will also increase your inner feeling of confidence and security which will likely enhance your confidence and ability in many other areas of your life. In fact, you will find you can apply many of these same principles to other aspects of your life and experience increased prosperity in multiple life domains.

Isn't prospering so much better than perishing, floundering, or barely getting by? Productivity is vital to surviving and prospering in your chosen profession, so it's worth spending some time to learn strategies designed to maximize your scholarly productivity. There are no guarantees in life, but being productive will all but ensure you prosperity in every stage of your academic career. Now that you're hopefully convinced that productivity will help you prosper, we can begin to discuss how to achieve it. So, what are the principles for enhanced productivity? Priorities, efficiency, and pitfall prevention (PEP).

PEP Overview

The key objective here is to obtain what I have described as principles of enhanced productivity. You do this by building a "PEP mansion" to house this prosperity. This includes a strong foundation of priorities, walls made from efficiency, and a roof of prevention against the pitfalls that will rain down on you. I have created a model that summarizes these strategies (see Figure 0.1).

As you can see, having the right priorities is the foundation principle for enhanced productivity, after which comes efficiency and prevention. Part I describes issues relating to priorities and motivation. Part II describes how to increase your efficiency while managing several ongoing projects. Part III addresses common productivity pitfalls and how to avoid them. Finally, Part IV gives specific tips for enhancing PEP during early stages of an academic career. I will now provide a more detailed overview of each part.

Priorities: Part I

Prioritizing research and writing is crucial for achieving academic prosperity; in fact, it's the foundation of my framework. In Chapter 1, I discuss priorities, how to prevent the urgent from overtaking the important, and how to make research both urgent and important. In Chapter 2, I describe the

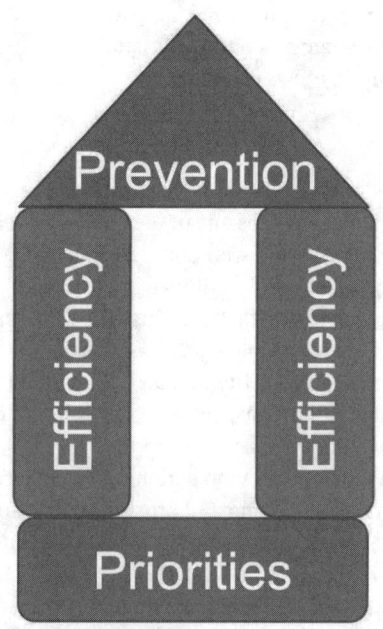

Figure 0.1 Principles of Enhanced Productivity

importance of selecting a research topic about which you can be truly passionate. I also discuss the importance of focusing on a limited number of topics in your research. Once you have found your passion, thereby increasing the perceived importance of your work, you need to enhance the urgency of research by setting concrete personal goals (Chapter 3). I also describe how being accountable to a weekly research goals group can add an extra zing to your motivation and urgency (Chapter 3). Finally, using existing deadlines and creating some of your own will light the fire of urgency within you (Chapter 4).

Efficiency: Part II

Once you have the correct paradigm, a topic you are passionate about, and have channeled and enhanced your motivation through goals, it's time to talk about building the walls of your prosperity mansion through efficiency. You'll first want to become a more efficient writer by writing a focused introduction, filling in your outline, and following other writing strategies which I discuss (Chapter 5). You'll also want to strengthen your skills at managing several projects simultaneously (Chapter 6), and cut out any wasted time in the publication process by quickly commenting on coauthor papers and speedily revising and resubmitting manuscripts with invited revisions or rejections (Chapter 7). Efficiency in this process can be greatly facilitated by sharing the labor. By selecting the right collaborators and being a great collaborator yourself, you can connect with or form your own winning team (Chapter 8).

Pitfall Prevention: Part III

Like huge hailstones, productivity pitfalls will rain down on the mansion you are trying to build. To protect the prosperous contents of your mansion, you will need to build a roof. The roof of your mansion will be built with the best available pitfall prevention materials. Chapter 9 warns of certain personality inclinations from within that hamper our productivity, including procrastination, perfectionism, idealism, cynicism, and "know-it-all-ism." Each of these can throw scholars into a state of paralysis and halt production. Another internal pitfall is burnout, which I discuss in Chapter 10. All the progress you've made will be for naught if you get burned out; this chapter describes ideas for feeding the flames of motivation and avoiding potential burnout by "sharpening the saw" and maintaining a balanced life.

In addition to enemies from within, the high-tech world we live in presents us with a multitude of distractions from without—Chapter 11 describes how to overcome these challenges. Lastly, as you become more and more productive, you will inevitably encounter more and more rejection (Chapter 12). Rejection, if not handled correctly, can throw a wet blanket on your productivity fire. Learning how to deal with rejection is an important step along the path toward research stardom.

PEP at Different Career Stages: Part IV

Part IV provides different tips for different stages of your career: undergraduate, graduate, and professional. Up to this point, the book has been primarily targeted at advanced undergraduate/graduate students and untenured faculty members, without distinguishing between them. Here, however, more specific advice is given to different groups. Keep in mind though that you can benefit by reading all of them. For instance, current graduate students will eventually be interested in specific tips for faculty members, and most professors work with graduate students and will likely be interested in reading the chapters targeted to graduate students to gain some useful strategies for guiding their students.

Chapter 13 provides advice for advanced undergraduates about setting themselves up for a productive graduate school career by preparing a successful application and selecting the best mentor and graduate program. In Chapter 14, I describe some of the major flaws in the graduate school system in America that deceives students into thinking that completing coursework is the grand purpose of it all. Then, Chapter 15 describes the important interpersonal resource of mentorship that is crucial to productivity.

The next set of chapters in this part provides a guide for new professionals. Chapter 16 discusses ways to make a productive transition to a first faculty position. In Chapter 17, I discuss the value of mentoring students and several strategies for doing it effectively. Chapters 18 and 19 teach how to be more time efficient in the roles of teacher and reviewer, respectively. Chapter 19 includes tips for excelling in your role as a reviewer while maintaining high levels of productivity. Chapter 20 sums up the entire book.

In sum, my objective is to help you prioritize research and to create and sustain motivation for research as a key priority (Chapters 1–4), increase the efficiency of your work (Chapters 5–8), overcome some of the pitfalls to your productivity (Chapters 9–12), and thrive at each stage of your research career (Chapters 13–20). I hope you enjoy this exciting journey!

Part I
Priorities

Priorities are the very foundation upon which you will build your prosperous PEP mansion. Putting research as a high priority will generate the motivation and provide you with the time you will need to make all the rest happen. You will learn how to put first things first (Chapter 1), how to choose a topic you find compelling and important (Chapter 2), and how to enhance the urgency of your research priority with goals (Chapter 3) and with deadlines (Chapter 4).

Figure 0.2 Principles of Enhanced Productivity

1 Put First Things First

Main Chapter Points

- We trick ourselves into thinking research is our top priority when often it is not.
- We fear obstacles of the publishing process and must overcome these fears by courageously passing through the "fire swamp."
- We fear other things will go by the wayside if we prioritize research, but we really *can* do it all.
- Set aside a specific time and place for daily writing.
- Tune out distractions.
- Set goals and make yourself accountable.
- Delight in deadlines.
- Choose a topic you find interesting and important.

Chapter Introduction

> Evan knows how important publishing is; his career depends on publications! He feels like it is a priority for him; however, by the end of the week he rarely has done much of it. Where does all the time go? As a graduate student, there are many competing priorities and each of them seems much more urgent than research. He is accustomed to getting straight A's and doesn't want to lose his great track record. As a result, his coursework always comes first and he spends a great deal of time preparing for classes. After all, they always say you should spend three hours outside of class for every hour in class, and Evan does at least that. Next, he has a teaching assistantship, and this usually takes up far more than the 10 hours it is supposed to take. Once he's done all of these time-consuming tasks, there simply isn't much left for research. Plus, Evan would admit that he's still reeling from the sharp, harsh words from the reviewers in the first manuscript he submitted, which was rejected. He's been enjoying the thrill of getting straight A's in graduate school and

> likes the positive feedback he gets from his students, which makes him feel valued and successful. Evan realizes that part of the reason he struggles to get to the research is because he's reluctant to face the rejection and harsh criticism he encountered last time, especially when he gets so much positive feedback from these other, more urgent tasks.

The foundation for my productivity framework is priorities. If research and writing isn't the number one priority of your work day on most days, you will not likely achieve academic prosperity. I believe the primary reason for lack of publishing productivity is that it is not truly of top importance for many scholars. Most academics, if asked, would say research and publishing is a top priority for them, but the reality and hard data prove that, for most, this isn't actually the case. One study by Boice (1989) found professors thought they were working an average of 58 hours per week and researching an average of 31 hours each week. However, when they were required to report their time in 15 minute increments, reality showed a much different picture. The average professor was actually not working 58 hours but a mean of 29 hours! This shows that we often think we're working a lot more than we actually are. However, even more alarming was these professors estimated they were spending 30 hours a week on research, while their actual self-report data showed they spent only 90 minutes researching, and only 30 minutes writing!

Of course you may say, "Oh that may be the case with *those* academics, but I'm different." However, I challenge you to track every 15-minute increment of your time in a time diary this upcoming week and see where you stand (see Appendix B). It may be a revelation to you to discover a discrepancy in where you think you are spending your time and what is actually happening with your time.

So what is going on? Why are many academics so misappropriating their time and energy? What is going on with their priorities? It's called self-deception. Many academics think they have their priorities straight and that they are putting enough emphasis on their research, but clearly the data suggest a different reality. So what can we do to change our priorities? I'm convinced that for research to actually become a top priority, we need to increase our perception of it being both important and urgent.

If you are reading this book, you are likely ahead of the game in realizing how important research and publishing are. Earlier in the book we discussed how publishing is the top item people look at when deciding who to hire, who to give tenure to, who to promote to full professor, who to give raises to, and so on. Though you're likely ahead of your peers in understanding the importance of research, we all have room for improvement.

Even more notable than perceived importance of research, many scholars lack a sense of urgency toward research. Many other things that appear to be more pressing than research are constantly competing for your attention. Without enough urgency, no amount of perceived importance of research will compensate, and you won't ever reach your full productive potential. In the next

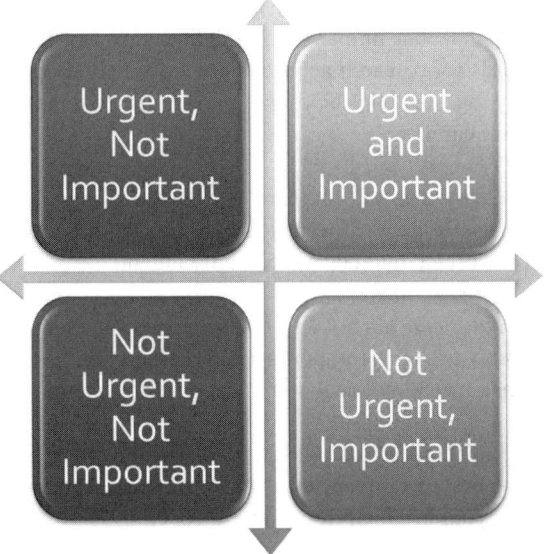

Figure 1.1 Urgency and Importance Matrix (Covey, 1989)

section, I will illustrate the interplay of importance and urgency by describing four quadrants in which we spend our time.

The High/Low Importance and Urgency Quadrants

"Life is composed of the urgent, the important, and the trivial. We exhaust ourselves on the urgent, seek rest in the trivial, and forget the important" (Webb, 1996–1999, as cited in Gray, 2010). Unfortunately, we spend a great deal of our time taking care of urgent matters that are of little importance. Covey (1989), author of bestseller *The 7 Habits of Highly Effective People,* suggests there are four quadrants in which we spend our time:

Q1: Urgent, Important. This category of tasks takes up perhaps the most of an academic's time. After all, something like teaching occupies an important aspect of an academic's life, and the urgency of a class lecture that has not yet been fully prepared can make it difficult to get around to research. Part of the problem is the task at hand usually fills the amount of time you allot to it. Thus, the urgency of something like teaching often trumps research in time spent. This is also the case with citizenship endeavors and other things which are an important aspect of an academic's career and which also carry a great deal of urgency, therefore taking precedent over research time.

Q2: Important, Not Urgent. Unless your tenure clock is about to run out, research tasks are important, but not typically urgent. Unfortunately, by the time the tenure clock is about to run out or the job market season is approaching, it's usually too late to get things published anyway, so the sudden urgency is in vain. Not only that, but unlike the immediate reward of teaching a good lecture, the rewards for research activities are extremely delayed. Thus, there are some strongly ingrained obstacles that prevent us from making research an urgent focus in our careers.

Q3: Urgent, Not Important. For researchers, this quadrant may include things like much of what you get with email. Many of the meetings academics sit through are not important, but they are certainly urgent.

Q4: Not Urgent, Not Important. This quadrant is comprised of tasks and distractions that aren't urgent or important. For researchers these may include surfing the Internet, checking Facebook, redecorating/cleaning your office, and the list goes on.

One objective of this chapter and ultimately of this book is to help you to put research in the first quadrant of urgent and important. You will only be able to fully maximize your productivity when this occurs.

Obstacles Preventing Research as a Priority

There are several obstacles that prevent us from making research a top priority. These include the fear of the many obstacles in the path to publishing, which I like to call the Fire Swamp, as well as the fear that other important things that are important will fall by the wayside as we prioritize research.

The Fire Swamp

Before reaping any rewards for research, one has to trudge through a great deal of perilous obstacles akin to those Wesley and Buttercup of the *Princess Bride* faced in the "Fire Swamp." Many of you recall this classic film from the late 1980s in which Wesley captured his true love and had to face the Fire Swamp in order to evade potential captors. After dodging the flame spurts and rescuing Buttercup from the quicksand, Buttercup says, "Wesley, what about the R.O.U.S.'s?" to which Wesley replies, "Rodents of Unusual Size? I don't think they exist" (*Princess Bride, 1987*). He is then immediately attacked by this brutal beast. Likewise, after dodging the flame spurts of the Institutional Review Board, the quicksands of our failed experiments or data that do not cooperate, we are then often attacked by two or three rodents of unusual size: bloodthirsty reviewers. And even after fending off all these challenges in the Fire Swamp, there's still a good chance we'll make it out of this swamp only to be met by Prince Humperdinck (a heartless editor) and an entourage of armed soldiers, be forced to surrender our manuscript, and begin the process all over again. Even if you're lucky enough to make it through unscathed, it will still be another 6–18 months before your work is actually published.

With this in mind, it is actually very reasonable that many scholars would choose to receive an immediate accolade from performing a committee task or from giving a good lecture to starry-eyed students, rather than face Prince Humperdinck and the R.O.U.S.'s. But somehow we have to delay our gratification and be willing to charge through the Fire Swamp with an unflinching determination. It takes some resiliency to not be deterred by the criticism and rejection inherent in academics. See Chapter 12 for more strategies on dealing with rejection.

Fearing Other Urgent Things Will Go by the Wayside

Another concern that prevents us from making research a top priority is an underlying fear that, by doing so, we will not be able to adequately juggle other important and urgent tasks, such as taking or teaching a class. Unfortunately, many graduate students and new professionals perceive research as a bonus activity to work on once they have completed everything for their courses. This is flawed thinking. The truly successful researcher learns to complete the research first, while attending to the coursework on the side.

The following is a metaphor that illustrates this point well, and you could even try it at home if you don't believe the pictures! All that is required is

Figure 1.2 Research Tasks Represented as Rocks and Other Urgent Tasks are Represented by Sand
(Photo by Bradley Gauthier http://www.bradleygauthier.com)

a glass jar, sand (or salt or whatever grainy substance you have on hand), and some rocks (or any solid objects). Here is what each object represents:

Jar = What you are capable of doing during a set time period
Sand = Coursework or teaching preparation
Rocks = Research

Class as the #1 prioritizer. The "class prioritizer" is represented by a jar in which the sand (i.e., coursework or teaching) was added first. They consider coursework or teaching to be the top priority and do that first, and they often "plan" to do research once all the coursework or teaching has been completed. Many sincerely *want* to do research, but grades and endlessly preparing lecture slides ranks much higher. These people will always put the sand in the jar first and then try to stuff rocks in during the "spare" time at the end. If you try this out, you will see that when the sand is entered first, you can't fit in many of your research rocks.

Research # 1 prioritizer. The "research prioritizer" is represented by a jar in which rocks were added first. This is the type of person who realizes that graduate school is not the prequel to their career, but actually the beginning of it.

Figure 1.3 The Class Prioritizer
(Photo by Bradley Gauthier http://www.bradleygauthier.com)

Put First Things First 9

Figure 1.4 The Research Prioritizer
(Photo by Bradley Gauthier http://www.bradleygauthier.com)

These people realize what they do now counts, and they are simply at a stage in their career in which they receive an additional benefit of "on-the-job" training with classes providing some additional guidance. Classes help the researcher understand the literature and to generate ideas for further research. Just as a salesman would not stop selling for weeks at a time while learning new sales techniques, neither does the "research prioritizer" stop doing what she was hired for—to produce research, while attending or teaching classes. If you try this out, you'll see when you add the rocks first you can comfortably fit all of them in the jar.

Magically, when you add the same amount of sand to the jar, all of it fits, despite the fact that there are twice as many rocks in this jar. The sand (or coursework and teaching) simply filled in all the cracks and empty space. At the outset it may seem as if the professionals who do their research first will not be able to adequately manage their coursework. "Research prioritizers" don't make the mistake of completely blowing off the sand. They attend to those responsibilities and usually do as well as the class prioritizers. But, by putting first things first, they are able to better accomplish the purpose of their graduate training—to become productive, independent researchers. Thus, putting research as a top priority does not exclude you from performing well in your other responsibilities.

Strategies for Putting First Things First

To maximize the quality time we spend on research and to stoke the flames of our determination to win the inevitable battle required for a publication, steps need to be taken. We need to enhance both our perceived importance of research as well as its urgency.

Set Aside Specific Time and Place for Writing Each Day

One way professionals prioritize research is to schedule blocks of time each day specifically for research or writing. I have a close colleague who religiously guards his "writing time" and does not answer any phone calls or allow any meetings to be scheduled during a three-hour block from 9:00 a.m. to 12:00 p.m. Having such a block of time set aside ensures other more urgent tasks (such as class deadlines) do not get in the way of what counts the most for your ultimate success as a scholar. Three hours may be a bit much to begin with, but I recommend setting aside at least some time each day in which you regularly write or engage in your research endeavors. Even if you simply get in the habit of writing for 15 minutes a day, that's a good starting point (Gray, 2010). If you become committed to a specific time each day no matter how busy you get, it becomes much more difficult to let other urgent activities knock you off your charted course. Having a set location for your writing may also assist you in actually accomplishing your goal, as it enhances the consistency of the exercise. My writing place is in a closed-off office in my home. I know that when I enter this room I am ready to write efficiently. It helps me get in the writing zone. Finally, I recommend starting earlier when you are fresh, rather than later when you are more worn out by other activities of the day. Not to mention that if your regularly scheduled time is later in the day, there's a much higher probability that other activities will crowd out this time.

I encourage you to keep track of the amount of time you spend in writing and the amount of words you write during each block. This can be a fun way to hold yourself accountable and to track your progress. You could even set a goal as to how many words you want to write in a set time frame.

Set Stretching Goals and Make Yourself Accountable

Setting goals that stretch you will provide urgency for your research. You may think, "I can't afford to get distracted by X or to do Y, because I'm behind on my research goals for this week." Even better is to make yourself accountable for your goals each week by forming a research goals group. Believe me when I say that knowing on Wednesday that you are going to go before your research group on Friday to report on your goal to submit manuscript x lights a fire of urgency under you (especially if you care about the opinions of those in your research goals group). I describe the urgency-creating potential of goal setting and accountability further in Chapter 3.

Diminish Distractions

Unimportant and non-urgent distractions vie for our attention on a constant basis. We live in a day in which these kinds of distractions have reached a pinnacle and bombard us in our email, Internet, phone, iPad, you name it. Some of these distractions can be urgent, but they are rarely important, at least in the long run. I devote an entire chapter (Chapter 11) to describing how we can diminish the distractions we face as professionals.

Delight in Deadlines

Reaching a weekly goal deadline that others hold you accountable for will provide urgency. Yet there are other deadlines you can take advantage of to add additional urgency to your research. For instance, if you are taking classes, make sure to heavily incorporate your research into your final paper for the class. That way you will have to push your research forward to meet that deadline. If you're teaching, you could write that you plan to lecture on your research topic (assuming it can be at least loosely tied into the course topic in some way), providing yourself a deadline by which you'll need to have carefully crafted your research ideas and have them ready to present. Chapter 4 provides other ideas for using deadlines to create urgency for your research.

Research a Topic You Care Deeply About

Choosing a topic to study you care deeply about is one way to enhance your perception of the importance of your research. If your topic is something you chose by default (e.g., "My graduate advisor wanted me to study this") or out of practicality ("I'm not really very interested in this topic; however, I heard I could likely get funding for doing this"), it will not likely matter to you much and, as a result, you won't be driven to make your research on this topic a high priority in your life. I cover this topic more extensively in Chapter 2.

Chapter Summary

A primary reason scholars aren't more productive is they trick themselves into thinking they are making research a top priority, when their actions show they are not. In fact, research is often considered to be an important but not urgent task, which is why academics struggle to spend the time on this task necessary for productivity. Fear of all the obstacles inherent in publishing and fear that other things will go by the wayside are obstacles to prioritizing research that need to be overcome. Setting aside a specific time and place for daily writing and diminishing your distractions during this time are important strategies for putting research first. Setting goals you are accountable for and delighting in deadlines will increase the urgency of research in your life. However, urgency of research won't matter much if the research isn't important to you. If you aren't studying a topic that gets you excited, you won't be motivated to achieve what you are capable of as a professional. I describe some key strategies for identifying a topic you are passionate about in Chapter 2.

> **Chapter 1 Wrap-Up Exercises**
>
> 1. When you don't have a deadline, which of the four quadrants of urgency and importance does research usually fall into and why?
> 2. What do you find (or think you will find) most intimidating about the research or review process? How might you overcome your fears?
> 3. What time of day and location would be ideal to block out for writing?
> 4. What can you change so research will always be both important and urgent?
> 5. Complete a time diary (see Appendix B) for a week to see how much time you are truly allocating to research.

2 Choose a Topic That Gets You Out of Bed in the Morning

Main Chapter Points

- Consider studying something you would want to study for free.
- Blend practicality with passion.
- Be programmatic in your chosen topic. Being programmatic will save you time in literature reviewing, data analysis, and grant preparation. It will also win you recognition.
- To maximize your productivity and motivation, consider being programmatic in two topics.

Chapter Introduction

> Jim graduated with a bachelor's degree without deciding for sure what he actually wanted to do for a living. His dad was a professor and had always pressured him to go to graduate school and get a Ph.D., so there he was. He selected a graduate program based mostly on its prestige and geographic location and didn't even take the time to look into the professors' research interests. When Jim began graduate school, he simply decided to study what his advisor was studying. This topic didn't really interest Jim much and so he didn't invest himself much in the research. He found he dreaded the time he spent on his research. He didn't enjoy reviewing the literature on this topic and found himself putting off tasks. Finally, Jim realized this path wasn't for him and applied to law school.

My dad was passionate about his job. I remember him always telling me the most important question to ask yourself when selecting a career is: "Is this something I would want to do without being paid?" I have found just such a profession! In fact, given that I typically worked much more than the hours that I was getting paid for during graduate school, I did like it enough to do it without getting paid. This passion was absolutely an essential ingredient for my success in publishing.

In fact, filmmaker George Lucas said, "You have to find something that you love enough to be able to take risks, jump over hurdles, and break through the brick walls that are always going to be placed in front of you. If you don't have that kind of feeling for what it is you're doing, you'll stop at the first giant hurdle." There are risks and several hurdles in this field and you've got to be passionate to break through them. If, like Jim, you find yourself dreading the time you spend doing research, you may seriously consider reevaluating the topic you're studying. You may be in the right field but are researching topics that aren't of interest to you (perhaps the research area of your major professor that isn't really your topic of interest). Academia is not for everyone—it's typically a low-paying job for the amount of training that is required (9–10 years minimum including your undergraduate education). So if you aren't excited about what you are learning in classes or the research you've been exposed to, you may want to seriously consider whether you are in the right field before you've invested even more time and resources. One recent article in *Business Insider* points out that about 80% of people hate their job, but most people decided on paycheck over passion (Shontell, 2010). John Seely Brown, former chief scientist of Xerox, stated in the article, "In a world of mounting economic pressure driven by intensifying global competition, passion is essential to the kind of performance improvement needed to succeed" (Shontell, 2010, p. 1). Like my dad says, consider if research is something you would love to do without getting paid. The field is oversaturated as it is, and it's extremely difficult to get a job these days. Plus, if you don't really like what you are doing, you are probably unlikely to excel enough to actually be competitive.

Selecting Your Topic

My sense is if you are reading this book, you probably do like what you are doing, or at least think you will like it. So, if you feel like you've successfully chosen the right field, the next step is to make sure you are passionate about the topic you are researching. It could be your advisor is dogmatic and expects you will research exactly what she researches; however, this is usually not the case as most advisors allow at least some flexibility. I suggest selecting a topic you feel passionate about, or switching topics if you are already a professor who has been in the field for a while. It needs to be something that gets you out of bed in the morning.

One way to choose a topic is to think of something that has some personal relevance to you. Also, think back to which undergraduate topics or courses perked your interest and see if you can do research in that area. You could peruse the top journals in your field and read the abstracts while asking yourself, "Could I see myself conducting these kinds of studies?" Read the future directions parts of the articles you find interesting and ask yourself, "Would I like to follow up on this suggested future direction?"

If you are in graduate school, it helps to choose a topic your advisor approves of and has background or interest in studying because she will most likely be a coauthor on your work (depending on your field). Additionally, the personal expertise of your advisor on the topic will be a helpful resource. Once you have found something you are excited about and your advisor shows some interest in pursuing, you can begin to plan out a systematic series of studies on the topic.

Mixing Practicality With Passion

Besides being passionate about what you study, you also have to consider how likely your topic is to receive funding. In an extremely competitive world, universities are increasingly interested in those who demonstrate potential to secure large grants. So factor this into the equation and talk to people in your department about the fundability of your chosen topic. One strategy may be to pursue two lines of research—one you are extremely passionate about and another that is more practical and will be more attractive to external funding. However, it's important to be programmatic in your research approach.

Building a Programmatic Line of Research

In general, I strongly recommend being programmatic in your research. In other words, your publications should build upon one another and should focus on one or two topics. Ideally you should make suggestions for future research in one manuscript and actually follow up and do what you suggested in the next study. There are several important advantages to being programmatic in your research:

1. **Saved time in literature reviewing.** You can become very familiar with the research literature in this particular area, which will save you a great deal of time in not having to search the literature as much every time you do a study. In fact, when I chose my topic of interest I wrote a very extensive review of every study I could find on the topic. Then, whenever I wrote a manuscript, I would draw on the references from my literature review in addition to checking if there were more recent studies published since my extensive literature review. This made writing the introduction sections of my manuscripts a snap. Just make sure you do not reuse the same language.
2. **Save time in data analysis.** Following up on your own studies also reduces the amount of planning, and you can reuse datasets that contain your variables of interest to answer later questions on the same topic. Thus, being programmatic is also more efficient in terms of data analysis.
3. **Grant preparation.** To secure research grants, it is important to demonstrate you have 'been around the block' and published a substantial amount of research on a given topic.
4. **Recognition.** A major indicator of success in academia is becoming known or recognized as a leading scholar in a certain area. You should be seen as an expert for a specific topic. In fact, this is a key requirement to being promoted to a full professor. If your research is scattered across too many topics, chances are you will never achieve high profile status in the field.

In summary, there are several advantages for being programmatic and developing a clearly connected line of published studies. One disadvantage to this approach is it can get a bit dull. However, there's no law against being programmatic in more than one topic (provided you have a lot of energy), but don't overextend yourself.

The Case for Building Two Lines of Research

Although it is very important to be programmatic in your research, investigating every nuance of one topic can get a bit dull after a while. Although I'd strongly discourage studying multiple topics, my approach for dealing with boredom was to be programmatic in two topic areas. Many semesters I have run two major studies; one was designed to build upon topic #1 and the other to build upon topic #2. Once the data is collected, I'd spend a great deal of time writing up a manuscript on topic #1 until I'd tire of that topic and then switch to writing up a separate manuscript on topic #2. I have found this incredibly refreshing. Let's face it, if you are getting sick of thinking, reading, and writing about something, you won't do it nearly as well or as productively. Thus, switching between topics can keep you motivated and excited to wake up and go to work. If you choose this route, it's best (though not a necessity) if you can connect your two topics somehow under one umbrella so your research doesn't appear to be disjointed. Also, you need to do a self-evaluation and determine whether you have the motivation and ambition to do an adequate job in more than one topic.

Chapter Summary

Motivation is a vital ingredient in productivity, and that is why it is so crucial to choose a topic that gets you out of bed in the morning. Also, if you actually want to be a productive researcher, you will need to put in more time than you are being paid for on your meager graduate student stipend (or university salary for that matter). So, when settling on a topic, you need to ask yourself, is this something I would want to study without pay? If the answer is yes, you're in business. Yet keep the practicalities of future funding potential in mind. Being programmatic in your chosen topic is also important; however, to maximize your productivity and motivation, consider being programmatic in two topics. Once you have a clear direction for your research, it is important to enhance the urgency of research and your personal motivation to accomplish it through goal setting. In Chapter 3, I discuss one strategy that is sure to increase the urgency of your research.

Chapter 2 Wrap-Up Exercises

1. Write about one or two things you found most helpful in this chapter that you want to apply to your career.
2. Write down three topics you find interesting:

   Topic #1_____

   Topic #2_____

   Topic #3_____

3. Write what appeals to you about Topic #1:

4. Write what appeals to you about Topic #2:

5. Write what appeals to you about Topic #3:

6. Now, rate Topic # 1 on the following dimensions (you should answer with an advisor or a more seasoned scholar for confirmation):

   Rate your overall enthusiasm when thinking about researching this topic:
   Very low 1   2   3   4   5   6   7 Extremely high

   What is the likelihood you could publish about and receive grant funding for this topic?
   Not at all likely 1   2   3   4   5   6   7 Extremely likely

   What is the likelihood your advisor/seasoned scholar would be willing/able to assist you in your study of this topic?
   Not at all likely 1   2   3   4   5   6   7 Extremely likely

7. Now, rate Topic # 2 on the following dimensions:

   Rate your overall enthusiasm when thinking about researching this topic:
   Very low 1   2   3   4   5   6   7 Extremely high

   What is the likelihood you could publish about and receive grant funding for this topic?
   Not at all likely 1   2   3   4   5   6   7 Extremely likely

   What is the likelihood your advisor/seasoned scholar would be willing/able to assist you in your study of this topic?
   Not at all likely 1   2   3   4   5   6   7 Extremely likely

8. Now, rate Topic # 3 on the following dimensions:

Rate your overall enthusiasm when thinking about researching this topic:
Very low 1　　2　　3　　4　　5　　6　　7 Extremely high

What is the likelihood you could publish about and receive grant funding for this topic?
Not at all likely 1　　2　　3　　4　　5　　6　　7 Extremely likely
What is the likelihood your advisor/seasoned scholar would be willing/able to assist you in your study of this topic?
Not at all likely 1　　2　　3　　4　　5　　6　　7 Extremely likely

9. Based on all these considerations and in consultation with my advisor/seasoned scholar, I have decided to focus right now on Topic #_____ for the following reasons:

   Reason #1_____

   Reason #2_____

   Reason #3_____

3 See the Vision
Setting Concrete Production Goals That Will Motivate and Inspire You

Main Chapter Points

- Goals provide urgency for research.
- Start by making long-term goals.
- Break down your goals into yearly, monthly, and weekly goals.
- Make a monthly manuscript movement goal to track your progress and provide clear structure to your goals.
- Hold yourself accountable to your goals by forming a research goals group or accountability partner to whom you will report your progress each week.
- Make a group manuscript submission goal to get the whole team working together toward a common end.

Chapter Introduction

> Gabriella was very goal driven. She knew what she wanted and pursued it fully. First, she clearly identified exactly how many publications she wanted to have by the end of graduate school. It was an ambitious goal, but she knew if she worked hard and applied herself, she could reach that goal. She broke down her long-term goal into manageable yearly goals and her yearly goals into monthly and weekly goals. At first her goals were unrealistically high and she wasn't able to meet them. However, over time she was able to gauge what she was capable of and set goals that were readily attainable. She also learned that when her goals were vague and weren't easily measurable, they weren't very motivating to her. To increase her accountability to her goals, Gabriella would let her advisor know what they were, and this motivated her to push herself harder to meet them. By the time she graduated, she was amazed at what she had accomplished.

In the introduction, I mentioned the transformative moment in my career when my advisor invited me to join him in the big leagues and glowingly described his student who had published 23 articles before graduating. I had decided to match that level of success and even wrote down this goal. The subconscious mind is amazing, and when you give it a clear image and clear instructions, it goes to work on your behalf. I ended up finding a way to graduate a full year earlier than I had originally anticipated and was still able to make it to my goal!

Setting Personal Goals

When you begin your graduate career or a new job, set a high bar for yourself. Expect greatness. If you come in with the expectation that you will do well and excel, you'll work harder to be a leader and to stretch yourself. Covey (1989) emphasized the importance of beginning with the end in mind. The first step in effective goal setting is to create a clear mental picture of where you want to be 5 to 10 years from now. Envision yourself as having achieved these goals. Make the experience as real as possible. Try to experience the emotions you would feel and take the posture you would have at that moment. The more vivid the imagery, the more it will become a clear marching order for your subconscious mind. It would be even better to create a "Vision Board," in which you find actual images that represent your long-term goals and put them in a place that is visible for you to see every day (Canfield, 2005). People who do this are much more likely to accomplish their goals as it makes the goals more salient in their mind and puts their subconscious mind to work on the task.

Set concrete production goals. Rather than setting a goal of publishing (something you don't have a lot of control over), I found that monthly submission goals for the year were most helpful; that way, if you have a down month you can make up for it the following month. I counted every new manuscript I submitted, every rejected manuscript I improved and resubmitted, and all manuscripts I submitted for an invited revision. Begin with lower goals you can achieve and then build your way up as you become more and more able to manage. Let's say in your first year you set a goal to submit one new or revised manuscript a month, and you were able to meet or exceed that goal. The next year you may consider 1.5 or 2 manuscripts a month. Keep increasing the amount of your goal each year as your ability and productivity is enhanced. The number doesn't matter so much as making constant, steady progress toward higher productivity. I make a list of the manuscripts I'm currently working on and also have a list of the upcoming months, and then I set priority goals of which manuscripts I'd like to submit at what time. This gives me a focus and translates into weekly goals and daily motivation.

Acting As If

One way to make your goals seem very real is to act as if they have already been accomplished. For instance, O'Hanlon (2007), author of *Write Is a Verb*, suggests that you actually write your present self a letter from your future self.

In this letter, he recommends you identify your writing dreams, tell yourself how you accomplished your dreams, tell yourself how others responded to these accomplishments, and give yourself some sage advice from the future. This kind of exercise will help make your future accomplishments seem very real to you and will inspire your conscious *and* subconscious mind to go to work on how to make this a reality.

Accountability: Research Goals Group Meeting

Accountability for your goals is the name of the game for catapulting your productivity to new heights. Boice (1989) conducted a study in which he assessed three groups of professors: one which wrote in large blocks of time, another which kept daily records of their writing (e.g., how much time they spent writing each day), and a third which kept daily records and held themselves accountable to someone by reporting about their daily writing each week. You'll be astounded by the difference in the groups in the number of pages written or revised per year: 17 pages by those who wrote during large chunks of time, 64 pages by those who kept daily records of their writing, and 157 pages by scholars who kept records and were held accountable for their writing. That's quite a difference! In other words, those who kept a record and were accountable were 9 times more productive than those who wrote during large chunks of time and more than doubled the productivity of those who simply kept a record. Accountability can make all the difference. Below are some specific strategies for creating these accountability goal groups.

Paul Silvia (2007), in his book *How to Write A Lot* (which I highly recommend), suggests forming a writing group that meets weekly to discuss writing goals. As I've tried this out, I've found that broadening it to research-focused goals has been helpful as many researchers don't currently have a project at the stage where writing is required. Make sure the focus of the meeting is on research goals since the point of the meeting is to push your research forward. The impact of the meeting can easily become diluted with class goals or teaching goals, which is why the focus needs to be on research goals.

During the first week, I recommend having everyone begin by writing their long-term, five-year goals. Knowing the big picture of where you want to end up will get you motivated to make the smaller goals along the way. I would then list out some of the one-year goals and challenge the group to make the goals quantifiable so you can clearly discern whether or not the goal has been achieved.

After that, you can all make goals for the week (with the end purpose of taking the steps necessary to reach your longer-term goals). Again, the key for these weekly goals is to make them very concrete and quantifiable so it will be very clear whether the goal has been achieved. The deadline for achieving the goals will be by the next meeting (preferably the following week at the same set time, though meeting every other week could also work).

During the meeting, one person should write down (or type out) all of the weekly goals as set by each group member. This is important as it provides a public record of the goals so individuals can't modify their goals midweek to fit their achievement. During subsequent meetings, each person reports how they did in achieving their goals and then describes their goals for the upcoming week. In fact, the writing of this portion of the book has been motivated by one of my research goals this week, which was to write 30 pages in this book. It's Tuesday morning now and I have written 12 pages so far, and I have until Friday at 12:30 p.m. to write another 18 pages. You can see how I'm personally being motivated by the accountability I have with my research goals group.

The thrust behind the research goals group is twofold: (1) to create accountability for your goals (having your feet held to the fire each week), and (2) to be a support group so you can feel rewarded when you achieve your goals. My current research group applauds each person following their weekly report (which may or may not fit the personalities in the group you will create). I must admit that I plan to finish writing the next 18 pages to meet my goal this week so I'll feel fully deserving of my group's applause. It really is a great feeling.

It is important to keep these meetings brief (between 30–45 minutes) because heaven only knows students and professors are already beleaguered with enough meetings. Thus, I would recommend keeping the group small (probably no more than 5–7 people) and don't discuss the details of the projects you are working on as this can start to chew up a lot of time. Nonetheless, a side benefit of these meetings is you can become familiar with the basics of the projects fellow faculty members or students are currently working on, which can facilitate collaboration. Another side benefit is you can be motivated and inspired by the efforts of others and even get ideas of goals you may adopt for yourself during these meetings. In my meetings, we also take the opportunity to discuss some things we can do to improve as scholars (e.g., discussing principles from this book).

If you struggle to find fellow students or colleagues who are interested in doing a research goals group, an acceptable alternative would be to simply find one person (it could be someone who doesn't know anything about research) and ask that person to be your accountability partner. I imagine there are online communities organized for this purpose. This could even be someone who lives far away. The key point is you need to report your goals and your progress (in person or by email, phone, or text) each week. Simply sharing your goals and feeling accountable will boost the urgency you have to follow through.

Teamwork and Group Goals

If you want to really motivate each other and foster accountability, you'll make a group goal. In fact, some researchers reviewed several articles on group goal setting and found that specific "group-centric goals" (maximizing individual contribution to the group's performance) had a positive effect on individual achievement (Kleingeld, van Mierlo, & Arends, 2011). Ask each group member how many manuscripts they think they could submit to a journal by a specific date. My group used a 5-month span with the end date being a month after the end of the semester, as a lot of other things come up that can hamper goal achievement at that time. Set a group goal to submit X journal articles by Y date. Our group of seven students in my lab met for the first time in January and everyone felt up to the challenge of submitting two new manuscripts by the end of May (14 new submissions). I asked our advisor if he'd be willing to take us out to dinner at a nice restaurant if we were able to meet our goals and he enthusiastically agreed. Having this group goal motivated and inspired everyone, and I'm pleased to report that we exceeded our goal and submitted 16 new manuscripts by the end of May. This type of group goal fosters unity and enhances the team spirit of 'your success is my success.' If you are a student, you may consider asking your major professor if she/he would be willing to provide some kind of incentive. If you are a professor, you may consider checking if your department chair might be up for providing an incentive.

Chapter Summary

Start by making long-term goals as a way to begin with the end in mind (Covey, 1989). Then break down your goals into yearly, monthly, and weekly goals. Consider making a monthly manuscript movement goal to track your progress and provide clear structure to your goals. Hold yourself accountable to your goals by forming a research goals group to whom you will report your progress each week. Also, consider forming a group manuscript submission goal to get the whole team working together toward a common end. Goals can be empowering and will motivate you to achieve success you didn't think was possible. Now that you have adopted the right paradigm and are motivated by your research topic and your goals, I'll discuss one other way by which you can generate urgency for your research—delight in deadlines.

Chapter 3 Wrap-Up Exercises

1. Write about one or two things you found most helpful in this chapter that you want to apply to your career.

Five-Year Professional Goals

2. Think of where you would like to be professionally in five years and list three measurable, concrete goals to help you get there.

   Goal #1 _____

   Goal #2 _____

   Goal #3 _____

One-Year Professional Goals

3. Now break your 5-year goals down to goals for this year that will build up to your 5-year goal.

Goal #1 _____

Goal #2 _____

Goal #3 _____

Monthly Professional Goals

4. Now, think of what you need to accomplish this month to accomplish your yearly goal.

    Goal #1 _____

    Goal #2 _____

    Goal #3 _____

Weekly Professional Goals

5. Now, think of what you need to accomplish this week to accomplish your yearly goal.

    Goal #1 _____

    Goal #2 _____

    Goal #3 _____

    Put these goals somewhere you will see them every day.

Research Goals Group

6. Write down the names of five people in your lab, department, or university you think may be interested in joining you in a research goals group:

    Person #1 _____

    Person #2 _____

    Person #3 _____

    Person #4 _____

    Person #5 _____

7. Write down some ideas for a realistic but challenging goal you could strive for as a group.
8. Write a few ideas for a potential reward for meeting your goals (e.g., going out to dinner, renting a house on the beach).

4 Delight in Deadlines and Accountability

Main Chapter Points

- Most people are motivated by deadlines and reach their peak production right before a deadline.
- Utilize the deadlines of class projects and conference proposals as tools to push forward the progress of certain manuscripts.
- Volunteer to present your research informally at a brown bag lunch setting or a group such as the Toastmaster's club.
- Letting others know about your personal deadlines provides additional accountability.

Chapter Introduction

> Tom used deadlines to his advantage. After the first day of class, he would examine his syllabus and particularly note the requirements for the final paper. He noticed that most of his professors left the topic somewhat open, so he would look carefully at the projects he had in their beginning phases and decide which one could be best advanced by that semester's paper. In some cases, he had already collected data that worked out according to his hypotheses, and thus he was able to use the class project to write the literature review for his paper and get feedback from his professor on his writing and organization. In other situations, the class paper he wrote helped him generate specific ideas he then tested empirically. He would discuss his ideas with his professors, and they were generally very supportive of using their course project as a springboard for published work. In fact, there were a few occasions when the professor became so involved and so helpful in the process that Tom invited the professor to contribute further to the paper and to be a coauthor on the manuscript the following semester. Tom's goal was to make every paper count double: to help him do well in the class and to assist him in furthering his research.

To procrastinate is common, and most people wait until a deadline to begin working. However, you can use these deadlines to your advantage. Most people are motivated by deadlines and reach their peak production right before a true deadline. There are some natural deadlines that are imposed in classes and by conference organizers. These can be used to full advantage to push your research forward in a significant way, but they aren't enough. In addition to the deadlines you are given, you should create additional deadlines and give them some punch of accountability through a research goals group. Let's begin by discussing how we can make the most of the deadlines that are already in place and then discuss how we can create accountability through reporting to coauthors, an advisor, or a research goals group.

Class Projects

In Chapter 2, I described how classes are far from the true purpose of graduate school. However, class projects can be effectively used to your advantage to push forward your research. Most graduate programs allow some flexibility in the choice of topic on the final papers. I recommend taking a careful look at the syllabus after the first day of class and plan out how you can best make it fit one of the research projects you are currently working on or one you are planning to do in the near future. Of course, ethics forbid reusing something you have done for another class, but it's not unethical to publish papers that started as a class project. However, going the other direction, like writing something for class you have published (with reviewer help) or that you have received several suggestions on from your advisor or committee (like a thesis proposal or dissertation prospectus), can be problematic and defeats the purpose of using the project to push your research forward.

If you communicate openly with the professor about your intentions early on, most will be supportive of trying to turn your project into something publishable. In fact, they may even give you extra help if they have that in mind. In any case, this kind of double dipping serves a dual purpose: it makes the time you spend working on a class project worthwhile and it provides a hard deadline to motivate you to make substantial progress on a manuscript.

Conference Proposals

Similarly, you can use the deadlines of conference proposals to provide motivation. I try to never submit work for a conference proposal that is already mostly completed, as it wastes a great deadline. Some conferences require the submission of a multi-paged proposal; this is helpful pressure for you to produce a lot of text in preparation for the conference submission. If your conference requires only an abstract, this can still be motivating to analyze the data in time to present it. Furthermore, preparing the actual oral or poster presentation can also push your manuscript forward.

Take Advantage of Less Formal Presentation Opportunities

Your university may have a regular forum for students or professors to be able to present their research, such as brown bag lunches or area meetings. Take advantage of such opportunities to push your work forward in a meaningful way. If these opportunities do not exist, or if they are sparse, you may consider forming your own informal group in which researchers present their ideas to each other. You could do this simply by talking to fellow graduate students or fellow professors and seeing who might be interested in doing a "research presentation" club. You could meet monthly or weekly depending on how many people are interested in presenting their ideas.

Another possibility is to join a Toastmasters Club—a public speaking group—which is something I did recently to increase the urgency of my research. You are given opportunities to speak on a regular basis and are allowed to determine your own topic. Although in this type of setting you would have to cut out some of the research jargon, it's a good opportunity to organize your thoughts and to present your research ideas in a way that makes sense to the layperson. This not only provides you with additional deadlines by which to organize your thinking and structure, but it could also help you better learn to communicate the "so what" of your research and make it understandable to a lay audience. This skill could help strengthen your ability to communicate to future editors about the value of your research. Another side benefit is you can get great feedback and help in your speaking skills, which can help you in your conference presentations. You can find a club near you on their website (http://www.toastmasters.org).

Creating Your Own Deadlines

If you are the type of person who is motivated by deadlines (and most of us are) you should consider making deadlines for yourself. In Chapter 3, I wrote a lot about personal goals; if you make these goals concrete and set dates, they can serve as helpful deadlines. However, adding an element of interpersonal accountability can significantly augment your motivation to complete your personal goals. A research goals group, as well as having a group goal (see Chapter 3), can provide just such accountability. In addition, you may find it helpful to share a manuscript submission target date with co-authors or an advisor, or promise to get an initial draft to them by a certain time. Adding the punch of accountability to others on your self-imposed deadlines will generate a level of motivation that may surprise you. Also, most people feel more accountable when they let someone in authority, such as an advisor or a supportive accountability buddy know about a deadline.

Chapter Summary

Most people are motivated by deadlines and reach their peak production right before a deadline. You can utilize the deadlines of class projects and conference proposal as tools to push forward the progress of certain manuscripts.

Also, planning ahead to maximize each class paper to be the foundation for a future publication will enhance your efficiency as a scholar. Volunteer to present your research informally at a brown bag lunch setting or a group setting such as the Toastmaster's club. Finally, deadlines of class projects and conference proposals may be insufficient, and it can also be helpful to let others know about your personal deadlines. Now that we have discussed prioritizing research by increasing its importance and urgency, let's move on to discussing how to maximize your productivity by building walls of efficiency.

Chapter 4 Wrap-Up Exercises

Write about one or two things you found most helpful in this chapter that you want to apply to your career.

List the writing assignments/final projects you have been assigned for your classes this semester.

Assignment #1 _____

Assignment #2 _____

Assignment #3 _____

Assignment #4 _____

Assignment #5 _____

Now, write how you can use each of these to push a specific research project forward.

Assignment #1 _____

Assignment #2 _____

Assignment #3 _____

Assignment #4 _____

Assignment #5 _____

Write down the deadline for the proposal of the next conference you plan to attend as well as what project you plan to advance with this deadline. If you don't have a project, how can you build on what you've already done to create new projects?

Finally, list these assignments you plan to turn into manuscripts.

Part II
Efficiency

You have now built the foundation to house the prosperity you seek. Although it's essential to have the time and motivation generated by having research as your #1 priority, these could be squandered without being put to efficient use. Efficiency is like the walls in the home you are constructing. There's no sense in building walls if you do not have a strong foundation, but your level of efficiency will determine how tall and grand your mansion will be. I begin in Chapter 5 by describing how to speed up the actual writing process. Chapter 6 illustrates the value of having several ongoing projects. Chapter 7 outlines how a great deal of time is lost during the internal and external review process and encourages a "hot potato" approach to handling manuscripts that are in your court. Lastly, Chapter 8 describes how collaborating with bright people can drastically increase your efficiency. These four chapters are crucial for building solid and impressive walls to house your academic prosperity.

As a reminder of the end goal we're working toward, here's the PEP model once more. Note those walls of efficiency:

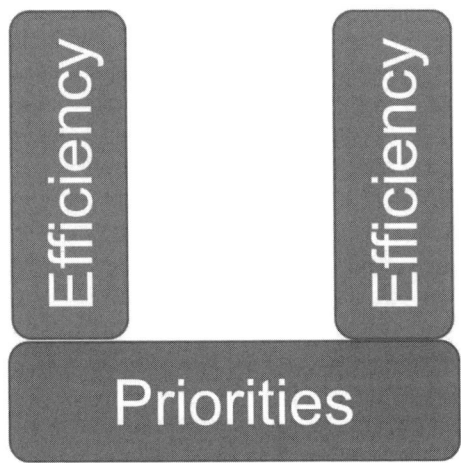

Figure 5.1 Principles of Enhanced Productivity

5 Speed Up the Actual Writing Process

Main Chapter Points

- Researchers often take much more time than is needed in writing.
- An introduction should derive your hypotheses, not review all literature on the topic.
- Read-to-write in order to reduce time spent in the literature and to write only what you need.
- Simplify your writing style to save time and improve the readability of your work.
- Keep your manuscripts as short as you can.
- To accelerate the pace and organization of your writing, try outlining, free writing, and writing to a model.

Chapter Introduction

> Phillip spent several months finding every article that was written on the topic of his research of prejudice—a vast literature. Once he felt like he'd covered everything, he felt comfortable beginning the writing process. He found it difficult to organize all the literature he read in a clear way, and it took him several weeks to synthesize all the literature on this topic in a way he felt satisfied with. The next problem he faced was that by the time he finished writing all the elements of the paper, it was too long for most journals. He could only find one journal that would accept articles of that length, and four months after submitting to this journal, it was rejected. One comment of the reviewers was that it was difficult to understand the purpose of the study from reading the introduction. Phillip's only option to resubmit the article was to cut the length significantly. He'd invested so much time reading and synthesizing this literature that he was reluctant to cut much. Deciding which elements of the paper to drop became a long, painful process for him.

Unfortunately, Phillip's situation is more common than we might think, especially for less seasoned scholars. Writing up your research the wrong way can consume so much of your time and your productivity. Be wary of this pitfall. Conversely, if you apply certain strategies at the beginning of the writing process, you will not only save yourself a great deal of time, but you will also make your writing more clear and readable. A few suggestions for making the writing process more efficient and time effective are to streamline your introduction, simplify your writing style, keep it short, outline the headings, write to a model, and free write.

Streamline the Introduction

One of the biggest time eaters in academics is endlessly searching through the literature and then turning the introduction into a comprehensive review of everything that has ever been written on the topic. This is NOT the purpose of a good introduction, but is, unfortunately, what many people have been taught. The primary purpose of the introduction is to derive your hypotheses. Essentially, all you need to do in the introduction is cogently make your case for why you think A is related to B. Don't bore the reader and waste your own time by describing everything you know and everything that was ever written about both A and B.

Another common problem with introductions is authors spend way too much time introducing concepts before they let the reader know what the purpose of the study is. State the purpose by the end of the first page at the latest and perhaps even by the end of the first paragraph. Doing so will not only assist the reader in understanding the aim of your article early on, but will also help you be more focused as you will try to demonstrate how everything you are writing applies to your topic. These can be difficult changes to make as most papers for graduate classes are not written this way; thus, it becomes a matter of changing your paradigm.

Read-to-Write. Perhaps one of the best strategies for streamlining your introduction is discussed by Gray (2010) in her book *Publish & Flourish*. She points out that the typical approach is to read all the literature and then write it all up. Instead, you should read-to-write, or in other words, you should make the points that support your research findings and then read the literature to find the evidence to help support your point. For example, you may write something like, "Nearly half of all marriages end in divorce (cite)" and then go look for the citation at a later time. You'll be surprised to find that as you make well-reasoned arguments, you can usually find evidence to back up your claims after the fact. However, be open-minded as you fill out those citations as there are times when the research actually supports the opposite conclusion. In fact, you should also examine the literature in search of research that does not support your research findings. Don't gloss over or ignore the contradictory evidence or your reviewers will call you out on it.

Taking this approach will help you to include only that which you need to make a strong case for your study. When you've already spent a great deal of time researching the literature and writing a lengthy introduction, it can be emotionally painful to trim down writing you have spent so much carefully crafting. Thus, it's much better to simply write what you need from the beginning.

Sometimes, when we research the prior literature too heavily, it can diminish our confidence and make us question what contribution we may have to offer to the topic. Martin (2011), author of *Doing Good Things Better*, advocates the read-to-write approach when he states:

> There's another, more practical reason why writing first—before doing the research—is more efficient than writing only at the end. Let's say there are ten major books in the area you want to write about. The normal approach is to read them first, and probably you'll want to read even more books and articles just to be sure you understand the topic.
>
> This approach can lead to a reluctance to start writing: the more you know about the topic, the harder it is to measure up to all this work by prior authors. . . . When you write first, before doing all the reading, you find out exactly what you need to know. In writing an article or chapter, you find gaps in your argument, points where you need examples, and places where you need a reference. So when you turn to the ten books, you don't need to read them in full. You'll know exactly what you're looking for, so you can just check the relevant bits. (2011, pp. 22–23)

I think this is important advice. Sometimes engaging too much in prior literature can diminish our confidence and make us question the contribution of our research. As a general rule, however, you should have read enough of the literature to know if your study has already been done so you don't waste your efforts.

Use a graveyard when needed. As I mentioned previously, it can be emotionally painful to cut things you've invested time into. Reading-to-write is a great way to reduce the amount of material you compose initially. However, even the most concise writer will inevitably revise their writing before their final draft. No matter how specific you keep your introduction at first, eventually, you'll want to revise and make further cuts to keep your introduction focused and concise. One strategy that can both help you feel better about shortening your manuscript and save things that might potentially be useful for a future draft or for another manuscript is to create a "graveyard" at the bottom of the manuscript or in a separate document (Gray, 2010). Simply cut and paste the things you delete into this "graveyard" and you will have them for later use.

Simplify Your Writing Style

One of the major problems people have in writing research papers is they attempt to use large, flowery words and make their prose sound very elevated and sophisticated. Sometimes we get the idea that as researchers we need to elevate to a certain level of complexity to be taken seriously. However, doing so has two major disadvantages: it takes longer to write in this style and it makes it harder for the reader to understand your main points. You want to aggravate your reviewers as little as possible. Writing in simple language will be easier for you and will allow your reviewers to whiz through your article, leaving them with a much more favorable impression.

The tradition of the past was to write in the third person, which leads to passively constructed sentences. Most disciplines have now embraced writing in the first person, which allows you to avoid the stilted passive tone of the third person and keep your reader more engaged. For instance, you can change the stodgy phrase like "The study was conducted. . . ." to "We conducted the study. . . ." with a simple voice change. Using language that is clear and easy to understand will make the reviewers and editors feel better about the manuscript. Of course, you don't want to use colloquial language, but allowing your voice to come through in your writing will make writing much easier (and faster) for you and for your readers.

Consider the following quote by C. Wright Mills:

> Such act of intelligibility, I believe, usually has little or nothing to do with the complexity of subject matter, and nothing at all with profundity of thought. It has to do almost entirely with certain confusions of the academic writer about his own status. . . . [Because the academic writer in America] feels his own lack of public position, he often puts the claim for his own status before his claim for the attention of the reader to what he is saying. . . . To overcome the academic prose you have first to overcome the academic pose. (1959, pp. 218–219)

Essentially, when you write in flowery language, you are trying to make yourself look smart at the expense of the reader. The primary purpose for writing should be to communicate ideas rather than to show off.

Keep It Short

Long papers don't do anyone any favors. Not only do lengthy manuscripts take much longer to write, but they also aggravate the reviewers and editors who have to read through them, leaving them with a negative perception of the paper. Additionally, editors are keenly aware of the limited space in their journals and will be more reluctant to publish something that is long as two papers could be published in the space one very long paper consumes. Do yourself, the reviewers, and the editor a big favor by keeping your manuscript short.

In fact, many journals encourage the publication of shorter reports. If your finding isn't very complex, you may want to consider submitting it as a brief report. The great thing about this format is it saves you a great deal of time in writing and (at least in my discipline) you get just as much credit for it as you would for a long monster paper! No one is going to look up your curriculum vitae and say, "Oh that manuscript was actually shorter than the typical article in that journal, so it shouldn't count for as much." Most scholars won't even notice or necessarily care about the length because they don't usually read entire articles, so it should give you as much credit as a full-length paper. If your research can be condensed, this could be an ideal option to maximize your productivity.

Outline Your Paper Using Headings That You'll Keep for the Manuscript

Most writers, I would argue, do not use enough headings. It's difficult to use too many and almost nobody does. Headings act as signposts, guiding your reader through the important points of your paper. Coming up with an outline before you write your paper can be extremely useful because it will help you determine the direction you want to take in your writing. Having it planned out beforehand not only helps you to gather the pertinent information you need to make your point, but it also helps you stay on track as you are writing. Without an outline it can be easy to lose focus and just write whatever comes to mind. After you plan your outline, you can simply use it as headings for your manuscript.

Write to a Model

I'm sure you have heard the phrase, "A picture is worth a thousand words." Indeed, a picture has tremendous value and is underutilized in academia. Why not create a conceptual model to pictorially alert your reader to the central point your article makes? I will often label different paths of a conceptual model with letters or numbers and then describe each path under a separate heading. This not only provides a great organizational summary of your central ideas for the reader, but it also helps you to more concisely describe your arguments. It can quickly organize your entire paper, greatly accelerating the writing process.

Free Write

If you don't know enough about the direction you want to take to make an outline, you might consider free writing, or just writing down your thoughts in complete sentences. Simply starting the writing process can get the wheels cranking and can help you in the thinking process. Sometimes just starting to write will help get the juices flowing and can help you to think more constructively about the topic.

Chapter Summary

A great deal of time can be wasted in the writing process. Following certain strategies will not only save you time and effort, but will improve the clarity and conciseness of what you are writing as well, making it more appealing to journal reviewers and editors. A common mistake is writing too much; remember, an introduction should derive your hypotheses, not review all literature on the topic. Read-to-write in order to reduce time spent in the literature and to write only what you need; graveyard anything less relevant. Simplify your writing style to save time and improve the readability of your work. Keeping your manuscripts short will not only reduce your writing time per manuscript, but will also make reviewers and editors happy. Outlining, writing to a model, and free writing can help you accelerate the process as well as improve the organization of your writing. Now that you know some tips for speeding up your own writing, you are ready to branch out and enhance your efficiency by managing multiple projects at one time as will be discussed in Chapter 6.

Chapter 5 Wrap-Up Exercises

1. Write about one or two things you found most helpful in this chapter that you want to apply to your career.
2. On a scale from one to ten, rate to what degree you are currently writing introductions to (1) review all the literature versus to (10) derive your hypothesis. If you didn't give yourself a high rating, what is your plan to improve in this domain?
3. On a scale from one to ten, rate to what degree you are currently writing with (1) complex versus (10) simple language. If you didn't give yourself a high rating, what is your plan to improve in this domain?
4. What strategy (e.g., outlining, free writing, writing to a model) do you think could help you to speed up and improve your writing? What is your plan to implement this strategy?

6 The Snow Fort Principle
Manage Several Ongoing Projects

Main Chapter Points

- Focusing on one manuscript at a time is highly inefficient.
- Have simultaneous projects in the works to help with motivation and efficiency and buffer you against rejection.
- Track your manuscripts with a charting system.
- The rule of three suggests you have at least one manuscript in the planning, executing, and writing/revising phase at all times.

Chapter Introduction

> Natasha believed in the need to begin a project and focus on it until it was completed. As a result, she focused all of her time and energy on her master's thesis. She first worked on getting her project approved by the Institutional Review Board (IRB). Unfortunately, the IRB was slow and requested several revisions. It took four months before she finally got her research approved, during which time she waited and worked on her class assignments.
>
> Once she finally got approval, she worked hard to prepare to run the study and train her undergraduate research assistants. Because the IRB took so long, however, she missed the chance to collect data in the spring and had to collect data over the summer. She didn't have enough participants over the short summer term so she had to continue collecting data in the fall. Once again, everything seemed to be taking longer than she'd planned and since she didn't have other research going on she tried to keep herself busy with coursework while she waited for more study participants.
>
> Finally, she had enough participants for her study. She was excited that her data analysis yielded results she thought could be publishable. She wrote up the results and sent the draft off to her major professor. Unfortunately, her professor was very busy with many different things and had several conferences to prepare for when she received Natasha's paper. Two

> months passed before she was able to give Natasha feedback for major revisions that needed to be made, and then she took another six weeks to provide feedback on the improved draft. After nearly six months of slow revisions, Natasha had to wait for the rest of the committee to look it over and give feedback before she eventually could defend it. Natasha finally submitted the manuscript for publication. The reviewers took five months before sending her a rejection letter. By the time she revised the article, resubmitted it to another journal, and began the waiting game all over again, it was time for her to enter the job market and her prospects were dismal. Surely this wasn't her fault; she was the victim of a series of unfortunate events, right? Wrong. In this chapter, we'll discuss how to avoid Natasha's fate.

It snowed every winter where I grew up in the Rocky Mountain West. Every time the snow fell, my brothers and I eagerly put on our warm clothes and headed outside to make snow forts. Now, a good snow fort requires a series of large snowballs and we would often have several snowballs going at once. Having multiple snowballs in the works was more efficient and would give us a needed break when one snowball was getting very large. Sometimes we'd roll one snowball for a while, get bored of it, start a new one, and then come back to the old one. Once we got the snowball to a roll-able size, we'd call one or two others to come help push together until we got it to the right size. Then we'd line them up and stack them on top of each other. Oftentimes, we'd even make two forts at once, for the purpose of later snowball fights.

Importance of Having Multiple Ongoing Projects

In this analogy, each snowball represents a manuscript. Each snowball is a different size and you are constantly pushing and building several snowballs at once. At a certain point in the process, you will call other collaborators in to help push and enlarge the snowball, preparing it to contribute to the fort.

The fort represents a programmatic body of research. A single manuscript on a topic is not that interesting; however, when you combine it with several manuscripts on the same topic, you can create something truly magnificent, and other scholars will take note. So why is it important to have several projects going at once?

1 Sustain Interest and Engagement

As I mentioned in Chapter 2, it is very important that you are programmatic in your research; however, there is nothing that says you can't be programmatic in more than one area. I initially had two primary interests in graduate school; the great thing about this was when I found myself becoming weary or bored with one area I could switch to my other focus. I found this extremely refreshing. Not only does switching between topics keep things interesting, but switching between individual projects within a topic can keep you engaged and motivated. However, it's probably better if you can connect these two topics in some meaningful way under one umbrella. Please refer to Chapter 2 for more complete coverage of this idea.

2   Avoid Being Held Up by Slow Coauthors

When you get a manuscript to a certain point, you will obviously send it to your advisor or other coauthors, but sometimes people can take a while to reply. In Chapter 8, I discuss some strategies to motivate coauthors to reply in a timely manner; however, sometimes it's out of your control. While this can be a frustrating experience, if you have several manuscripts in the works, it's not as stressful because you have plenty of other career-furthering research projects to work on while you're waiting. This might also help you to be a better collaborator because you won't get impatient or pushy with other coauthors. It's not as big of a hindrance to you if someone takes long because you have other research to work on.

3   Stay Busy During Lags Lag Time

Similar to point #2, when you have a lot of projects in the works, waiting months and months (and even years in some cases) to receive a decision on the manuscript you submitted is not going to slow down your overall progress. While you're waiting for a decision on manuscript A, you've been working on and have submitted manuscripts B and C just in time to start working on the revisions for manuscript A. There are other research processes that require a lot of time, such as collecting data, and if you have several projects going simultaneously you have other research to pursue while the data is being collected.

4   Lessen the Sting of Rejection

I devote an entire chapter to strategies for dealing with rejection. However, one of the beauties of having several projects in the works is that the fate of a single manuscript doesn't affect you emotionally as much; since you don't have all your eggs in one basket, you don't lose as much when one of those baskets breaks. Having several projects helps you not become too emotionally attached to one single manuscript, making rejection easier (see Chapter 12). There have been times when I've received a rejection and an acceptance of a manuscript in the same week, so I say with experience that the success of the one manuscript can help you feel better about the rejection of another.

5   Double Dip

Having multiple papers on a similar topic allows you to recycle some of the citations and articles you've written, which can speed up your production considerably. Of course, you'll need to be careful to reword and rework it so as to avoid plagiarizing yourself. If you collect your own data, having multiple projects going also allows you to test several hypotheses in one data collection session. Of course, you need to be cautious when doing this so you don't overload participants, or so one procedure does not conflict with or bias later procedures. Oftentimes, I wasn't too discouraged about one finding not working out because I had another one I was testing that did.

Tips for Managing Multiple Projects

Have you ever seen someone walking multiple dogs at once? Some dog owners seem to have things completely under control, while there are others who struggle to maintain control when things get exciting and either wind up tangled in their leashes or let go of them altogether. It's important to know your own limits and how many dogs you can successfully command simultaneously—especially during stressful times. Here are some strategies that have helped me to keep things on a "tight leash."

Manuscript Progression Chart

A useful way to keep track of the progress of multiple manuscripts is to use a manuscript progression chart. Although the specific phases may be slightly different depending on your field, I have included a copy of what I use in the exercises at the end of this chapter. You can also download a copy from my website (www.pepstrategies.com). This simple document contains a space to provide a brief description of each manuscript you are currently working on and then boxes to report your progress at each of the following phases: IRB approval, data collection, data analysis, initial write-up, initial coauthor revisions, initial journal submission, revisions, resubmission, and in press. Besides simply checking off the boxes as I complete each phase, I write the target date by which I would ideally like to check off that phase. Having these charts out in front of me (I hang mine above my office computer) keeps me motivated and organized. Note that due to rejections, one manuscript may pass through some of the phases multiple times.

Rule of Three

The rule of three suggests you should have at least one manuscript in each of three major phases: planning, data collection/analysis, and writing/revising/submission. If you put too much emphasis on one particular phase of the research, you will become un-balanced. For example, if you focus all your time and energy on planning and running studies, you may get some cool findings but nobody will know about them because you haven't published them. Also, if another researcher in your field found the same thing and wrote the paper before you, you're stuck. Beat them to the punch! Similarly, if you focus all your time and energy on writing, you won't have any other projects to keep you busy while you wait for coauthors and journals to respond to your manuscript. The most productive scholars are constantly coming up with new hypotheses to test, and continually collecting data (or preparing secondary data for analysis) to get ready for the next writing project. It's probably a good idea to start out with three manuscripts—one in each category. As your capacity increases, however, so should the proportion of manuscripts you have going at each phase. In the beginning it might be difficult to have three projects going at once, but you will get used to it. Once you get comfortable with the number of projects you are juggling, slowly push yourself further. Your manuscript progression chart will help you track this to help keep track of things and keep your work in balance.

Chapter Summary

There are several important reasons to have simultaneous projects in the works, ranging from motivation, to efficiency, to being buffered from rejection. Tracking your manuscripts with a charting system will keep you motivated and organized while maintaining a balance in the developmental stages of each project. There is so much time wasted in the publication process, and the next chapter illustrates how treating manuscripts like hot potatoes can make a huge difference in your efficiency.

Chapter 6 Wrap-Up Exercises

1. Write about one or two things you found most helpful in this chapter that you want to apply to your career.
2. Write out all the projects you are currently working on in the manuscript progression chart provided for download on my website (www.pepstrategies.com).
3. Count out how many projects you have at each phase of the publication process, whether it be the planning phase, data collection/analysis phase, or the publication phase.
4. List the ratio of manuscripts in each phase. Keeping in mind the rule of three, write what phase you may want to enhance to improve your balance.

7 Think "Hot Potato"
Eliminate Wasted Time

Main Chapter Points

- We can cut a lot of lost time and inefficiency out of the process of publishing by dealing with three "hot potatoes" before doing other work.
- First, respond to coauthors requests for feedback.
- Second, revise manuscripts that have a "revise and resubmit" decision.
- Third, resubmit rejected manuscripts.
- *Then* do everything else.

Chapter Introduction

> Jasmine just recently began a tenure-track position at a well-known university and has already gained a reputation among her students and coauthors for being slow to respond with feedback. This is beginning to cause problems and generate complaints. One of her students, Bill, sent her a manuscript 3 months ago, but she still hasn't found time to reply. She has found being a new professor to be a daunting task and feels overwhelmed. She has classes to plan, a new environment to get used to, graduate students to become acquainted with, and a department chair to please. How could she possibly take time to give adequate feedback when there's so much to take care of in getting started with a career? On top of all this, Jasmine had a manuscript rejected that was taking a long time to fix. It always seemed to take a while—sometimes a full year—to recover from the sting of rejection and finally get around to resubmitting it. In fact, she has two manuscripts that had been rejected early in her graduate school tenure, which she is still sitting on. As soon as she can settle down and find the time, she'll finally get around to it. How would you rate Jasmine's prospects for getting tenure?

Many of you are familiar with the game "hot potato." For those who are not, it works like this: the music plays and you toss an object around (like a bean bag) that represents a hot potato. The objective is to get that object (the "hot potato") out of your hands as quickly as possible to avoid having it when the music stops. This is a useful analogy for efficiently handling certain manuscripts during the publication process, with some manuscripts being hotter than others.

There are many inefficiencies in the current review system that we have no control over. For example, it depends on the field, but I'd guess the average time to receive an initial decision letter on a manuscript is 3 months, and that the average time from initial manuscript submission until acceptance for publication is 9 months. (Now that I am an editor, I realize much of the reason for this time is because so many people are unwilling to review manuscripts and it can sometimes take several weeks simply to find reviewers for a manuscript.) Likewise, I had one manuscript that took 10 months to receive an initial review of and another manuscript that took nearly two years from the time of the initial submission until it was actually published. Thus, there is obviously room for improvement in the current system, yet it is likely to stay like this in the near future.

However, there are several areas of wasted time in the publication process we do have control over. We can reduce the lag time from initially sending a manuscript to coauthors to the time we receive their feedback. We can quickly complete revisions. And we can get rejected manuscripts back out for review in good time. Besides discussing how to cut some of the fat out of this process, in this chapter I will identify the manuscripts I think are the hottest and most urgent to take action on.

Heat Index on Manuscripts

Certain documents should be treated like a hot potato in that you need to work carefully and methodically, but also swiftly to get them out of your hands. The idea, of course, is not to rush so much that you do a poor job, but to put this manuscript at the top of your priority list. The following is a "Heat Index" with the hottest manuscripts at the top, as well as tips for increasing the efficiency for each manuscript type.

Hottest: *Nearly polished manuscripts from collaborators.* I put these at the top of the heat index for a few reasons. Few things are more frustrating to a collaborator than having to wait a long time for a coauthor to send back revisions. Oftentimes, when a manuscript hits your inbox, it is pretty well on its way and just needs some touching up before being sent in. Be thorough in your response, but don't keep them waiting long. Your value as a coauthor will rise as you consistently prove to be both thorough and quick. For professors, the articles of students should become a top priority. For students, having to wait a long time to hear back from a major professor on a manuscript is disheartening and stifles progress.

You may ask, what control do we have over coauthors who are slow in responding? Sometimes, there is very little you can do. However, there are ways of increasing the efficiency of this internal peer review process. One technique I have adopted from one of my collaborators that works well is sending the manuscript to all coauthors at once. Give them a specific date by which you hope to hear back from them (this should be at least 10 days to respect their time and busy schedules), and ask them to "reply to all" when they respond. There are two reasons for this: first, it saves you the time of having to reconcile two sets of feedback into one file, and second, it serves as a reminder to all other collaborators of the paper on which you are requesting feedback. Oftentimes, people don't want to be the last one to respond, so seeing that another collaborator has already responded can light a fire under them. Of course, this doesn't always work, but it does help things move along more rapidly.

For those who have an advisor who takes a lot of time giving feedback, I suggest that if they don't reply in a reasonable amount of time (respect the very busy schedules of professors), request an in-person meeting to discuss the manuscript for the following week. This will often get things moving. If your advisor is continually holding back your progress, you may consider having a heart-to-heart with him and letting him know that you want to be productive and you value his feedback. For all you know, there may be some hidden issues. For example, your professor may feel your work has not been adequately developed when you've sent it. In any case, this type of open discussion will likely help the situation. If it does not and your advisor continues to be abysmal at getting you feedback, you ought to seriously consider changing advisors.

A student once told me how her advisor wouldn't reply to her manuscripts for several months or sometimes even longer. Because of this, she wasn't able to publish much, which has now left her with little prospect of getting a job. You don't want to be in her shoes at the end of your graduate program.

Second Hottest: Revise and resubmit manuscripts. Any time you get a revise and resubmit decision from a publisher, you should feel great because this means your work is good, you just have to make some changes. I have a very high success rate of acceptance after resubmission once I get this decision. Because the manuscript is often quite close to publication, it's a good idea to strike while the iron is hot and to get it back in while it's still fresh on the minds of the editor and reviewers. The strategy I suggest is to be particularly thorough with your revisions by including the actual comments of the editor and reviewers (verbatim) and replying to each point by explaining how you addressed it in your paper. I try to address every query if I can, but if you disagree or do not have the data to address the issue, describe your rationale for your decision in a respectful and comprehensive manner. As an editor myself I can say that this is extremely helpful, because then I do not have to go back to check if the author missed any important points that were raised. If you do a good job you'll likely have a publication to add to your vitae in no time. Of course, the best way to handle inefficiencies on these manuscripts is simply to put them as your top priority and go to work.

Third Hottest: Rejected manuscripts. Many people lose a lot of time and productivity by letting the sting of rejection get in the way of getting a rejected manuscript back under review. In fact, based on conversations I've had with many scholars, I estimate the average time it takes most professors to resubmit a rejected manuscript is at least 3 months. All of that lost time could easily be eliminated or reduced.

I recommend making some improvements, taking the suggestions that are realistic from the reviewer's suggestions, and then, unless you're going to collect more data to drastically improve it, get that baby back out the door. Try resubmitting it to a different journal within the same week of rejection. Some people think every recommendation should be rigorously applied, but my view is that the same concern may not even come up at all with another set of reviewers. If you or your advisor are unconvinced that it's important to address, or if it's one of those issues that can't be addressed without redoing everything, I wouldn't worry about it.

Also, some people think it is necessary to send out the revised manuscript to coauthors for comments. However, unless you made major changes that would benefit from feedback or you need assistance interpreting and implementing reviewer feedback, many coauthors don't want to be bothered with having to review a rejected manuscript that has undergone only minor changes. Instead, I suggest sending the decision letter to collaborators and asking where they recommend sending the manuscript next. In this same email, you could let them know of your intention to get it back under review soon and inquire whether anyone would like to see the revised draft before you send it back for additional review.

Many people procrastinate improving and resubmitting a rejected article because of the emotional pain involved. Despite the negative feelings it can bring, I think delving into the negative feedback and getting it turned around quickly actually helps in dealing with the rejection. This may be due to the rejection being an "unresolved memory." An unresolved memory is an unpleasant memory that may intrude into the consciousness due to "unfinished business" associated with the memory (Watkins, Cruz, Holben, & Kolts, 2008). Getting it back out the door makes it so this rejection stops looming over you. Successfully handling rejection is covered in a great deal more detail in Chapter 12.

As previously mentioned, many scholars take probably 4–5 months to resubmit an article for publication. I'd like to illustrate just how much time can be saved by being quick on the resubmission trigger using a story from my own career. I once had a very bad week in which I got four manuscripts rejected. I decided to put off the other priorities I had and got to work on carefully looking over the reviewer feedback and applying what I thought would help to improve the paper. I had all four articles resubmitted to different journals by the end of the week. Now if the average time to resubmit is, say, 3 months, I saved myself 12 months, or an entire year, by reprioritizing my time and getting the four manuscripts back under review in a week.

Chapter Summary

We can cut a lot of inefficiency out of the process of publishing by trimming down on the time we spend responding to coauthors requests for feedback, revising manuscripts, and resubmitting rejected manuscripts. These three types of manuscripts are the hottest potatoes because getting them out of our hands in a careful but quick manner gives us the greatest chance of winning the publishing game.

So far we've discussed successful internal ways of approaching research and several strategies for maximizing personal productivity and efficiency. The following chapter addresses how to take advantage of human capital—the most important outside resource for becoming an efficient, productive scholar.

Chapter 7 Wrap-Up Exercises

1. Write about one or two things you found most helpful in this chapter that you want to apply to your career.
2. Using your project tracker created in Chapter 6, make a list of your current projects. Then, based on the heat index described in this chapter, rank order your projects in terms of priority.

8 Find Good Colleagues and Become Everyone's Favorite Collaborator

Main Chapter Points

- Good collaborators are probably the most important resource for productivity.
- Look for productive, skilled, and critical collaborators who complement you well.
- To have great collaborators, you need to be a great collaborator yourself.
- Respond quickly and with constructive comments.
- Provide updates on the status of manuscripts and express gratitude.

Chapter Introduction

> Theresa was very sensitive, both with her own and other people's feelings. As a result, she surrounded herself with friends who were nothing but complimentary to her. This also factored into her choice of advisor, and she went with someone who had a reputation for being very sweet to all of her students and never abrasive. All of her committee members were like this as well: they were extremely positive about her work. Based on their praise, she fully expected the manuscript would easily be accepted and could not believe her eyes when she received the review—the reviewers were SO negative! She was blown away by their comments and how they rejected outright all of her hard work. How could her committee think her research was so good while the journal reviewers could only see flaws? She was completely disillusioned and wondered if she could ever gather the courage to submit something for publication again.

To become truly successful at publishing, you can't do it alone; you need to work in a team. Being a part of a strong team of researchers can enhance your productivity more than most anything else, and gives you the opportunity to have other bright minds contributing to and sharing your workload.

Why Collaborate?

There are many reasons for collaborating and the scholars who do it best will ultimately have the greatest amount of success in publishing. For one, those who effectively collaborate with others can share the workload, generating what I call a "passive income of publications." Furthermore, there is great synergy and idea-sharing that occurs through the collaborative process. Finally, in a field in which most of the productive effort requires long hours of isolation with no company aside from one's computer, collaborating can reduce loneliness and feelings of seclusion.

Passive Income: Share the Workload

Most books about strategies for becoming wealthy emphasize the importance of what is called "passive income." This is the type of income you accrue while you are asleep or doing nothing, including things such as real estate investment, mutual funds, online marketing, etc. Writers of these books claim that almost no one (except professional athletes and entertainers) gets seriously wealthy through their core salary alone. Rather, the wealthy become skilled at putting their money to work for them so they can constantly make more money without having to put in as much effort.

The same principles apply to becoming wealthy in the "coin of the realm" of publications. You have to figure out how to have your scholarly body of work grow and develop while you're sleeping. A very literal example of this principle occurred just recently for me. A Fulbright scholar studying in India (12.5 hour time zone difference) contacted me and wanted to coauthor a grant proposal. It was due in less than 5 days, yet it seemed like too good of an opportunity to pass up. So I worked on it all day (Mountain Standard Time) and then before going to bed I emailed the proposal to him. He had just woken up and worked on the proposal as I slept and sent it back to me. In this unusual way, we got a solid grant proposal submitted in less than 5 days!

Of course, this is an extreme example and you don't need time zone differences to capitalize on collaborating. The key is if you have several projects going on simultaneously with multiple collaborators, the chances are that on any given day your body of work is increasing without you even turning on your computer. I'm not saying that collaborating gives you a pass to be lazy or to take advantage of the labor of others; rather, it allows you to share the workload involved in getting your work published and multiply your time resources with those of your collaborators.

Synergy and Ideas

In addition to dramatically multiplying your time resources, collaborating can multiply your intellectual resources. I'm sure you have experienced a time when you were struggling to come up with an idea or to figure out a good conceptual framework, then met with someone else, began bouncing ideas off that person, and suddenly the two of you were able to come up with much more than you ever could have by yourself. The intellectual capital gained through collaborating is enhanced even more when you work with someone who has particular expertise in a specific topic. My collaborators have pushed me to design studies I would never have imagined on my own. I have been able to publish articles in journals I otherwise couldn't have without the extra push and guidance from these collaborators.

Reduce Isolation and Loneliness

Let's face it: being a scholar is not an inherently social job. Being productive requires long hours of seclusion, typing in front of a computer. I think this is partly what hinders the productivity of most scholars—they get bored and lonely as they sit in isolation. As a result, they may get distracted doing other things that are time-wasting and unproductive. At the right time and place, these outlets can be refreshing and much needed. However, if you collaborate with a wide range of individuals, you can meet and discuss issues relevant to your work, thereby satisfying some of your social needs while also being productive with your work. In fact, I read that Pixar employees came up with *Cars*, *Monsters Inc.*, and *Finding Nemo* while talking during their lunch break. You have to eat lunch anyway, so you might as well give yourself a chance to generate ideas with colleagues, and who knows? You may come up with the next scientific breakthrough during your next lunch break.

Finding Good Colleagues

There is a difference between having a personal relationship with someone and having a professional, collaborative relationship. I definitely think it's a good idea to make as many friends as you can both in your department and in your field. However, you'll want to be a little more selective about those with whom you form a professional, collaborative relationship. Identifying the "right" people to collaborate with is crucial. Here are a few things to look for in a collaborator.

Productive Track Record

You want to work with someone who has a good track record of publishing frequently and in well-respected journals. Teaming up with someone who has the skills, insight, and abilities to conduct and write up high quality research will not only help you to succeed in publishing, but will teach you important lessons that will help you develop as a scholar. Past success is the best predictor of future success, so be on the lookout for these "proven" individuals and strive to be the type of scholar who would attract the interest of this type of person.

Statistical Savvy or Some Other Skill

Unless you are a whiz with statistics, you may benefit from seeking out someone who has these skills. Continual advancement of statistical sophistication has certainly raised the bar for publications. Procedures that were the gold standard 10 years ago are often viewed as insufficient by some of the leading journals today. It's good to connect with someone who has the statistical savvy to help you with the analysis; however, it's even better if this is the type of person who is good at explaining and will take the time to sit down with you and teach you how to do it. I've taken eight graduate level stats courses, and I can say without hesitation that almost everything I actually remember, I learned by someone demonstrating it for me outside of class and then having to do it for an actual publication. If your field doesn't use statistics, you may consider teaming up with someone who possesses savvy in whatever methodological skills may be relevant in your field. Of course, you not only want to benefit from others who have skills, but learn the skills yourself so you have more to offer future collaborative partners.

Complement of Your Style

You know what your strengths and weaknesses are as a writer and as a researcher. It can be very helpful to find someone who will help you fill in the gaps where you lack. For instance, O'Hanlon (2007), author of *Write Is a Verb,* described a collaborator who was much more detail oriented than he, which really helped during the editing process. Finding someone with a different style can be very beneficial. When you find someone who is strong in the areas in which you are weak you are able to get much more accomplished.

Critical Mind

A friend of mine told me about a renowned scholar in his department who had a lot to offer. However, he had a reputation for being rude and tended to scare students. I'm aware that several students avoided working with him or asking him to be on their committees because of his reputation. These students deprived themselves of a great learning opportunity. Don't run away from people who will be critical of your work; rather, embrace them. Many collaborators are afraid of hurting your feelings and are hence reluctant to tell you what they actually think of your work, leaving you instead with editors or reviewers tearing it apart and rejecting it for the same issues that could have been resolved "in house." What worth is a collaborator who simply pats you on the back and perhaps fixes a few typos? Value the person who will be critical. This is the only way you will improve not only a specific research article, but as a scholar in general. Getting used to criticism will also help with getting hired—when giving your research talk during a job interview, you can't be intimated by questions or criticisms leveled against your work. Unfortunately, some critical minds are not very good at giving feedback in a constructive manner; however, I would still prefer this type of person to a "back patter." Sure, in the short run you may prefer a "back patter," who may help you feel good about work or yourself, but the critic will always prove most valuable to you as they will prepare you for the professional world.

I once sent out job application materials to my team of eight undergraduate research assistants, hoping they might have some suggestions (at least for writing) that could improve my materials. I must admit I was extremely disappointed because nearly all of them wrote back and said everything looked great. Needless to say, their feedback was not at all helpful to me. There was one research assistant who made several comments, corrections, and suggestions. I think she was a little nervous that she had offended me; however, her feedback had the opposite effect. I was so thrilled by her critique that I offered her a promotion! Never be afraid to offer constructive criticism when people ask you to look over their work because that's what they are asking for! Although my other students were trying to be nice, none of them did what I had asked, which is why I was so pleased with the one student who actually did offer constructive criticism.

However, good feedback is useless if you don't apply it. One expert wrote, "Listen to what your reader says as though it were all true. The way an owl eats a mouse. He takes it all in. He doesn't try to sort out the good parts from the bad. He trusts his organism to make use of what's good and get rid of what isn't" (Elbow, 1973, pp. 102–103). You ought to take in all the feedback you get like a sponge, and trust you'll know what you should ultimately keep and what you don't need.

Where to Find Collaborators

Now you know some things to look for, where do you find such people and how? There are a few different ways. You may start in your department as you will have frequent contact with these colleagues and are more likely to find others interested in your same topics. However, there may also be great colleagues awaiting you in sister departments within your college. Check them out online and, if you can, talk to someone who has worked with the person you might be interested in connecting with to ensure you aren't walking into a minefield.

Additionally, don't limit yourself to the boundaries of your own university. Conferences can present an opportunity to find colleagues who are interested in your topic. I suggest you do a little background research on some of the people you're interested in connecting with and they will be flattered when you mention having read a specific article they wrote. Attend their oral or poster presentation and ask some meaningful questions. It's always best to first show interest in what they're doing and they'll be more likely to hear more about your research and what you might be able to bring to the table in forming a collaborative relationship. If things go well during the initial interaction, don't be afraid to ask them if they want to get a drink or talk more about an idea over dinner.

However, don't be too surprised or discouraged if nothing actually comes of it. Sometimes people say what you want to hear or may have some interest, but when they get back to the grind of all their current projects with people they see on a frequent basis, your shared project with them can quickly become less salient. Definitely follow up with these people, but don't be offended if the planned project doesn't materialize.

Becoming Everyone's Favorite Collaborator

You may have heard the phrase, "To have a friend, you've got to be a friend." Well, to have great collaborators, you've got to be a great collaborator. Here are some ideas to help you be the collaborator other collaborators will want to have on their team.

Be Prompt

The best people to have on your collaborative team are those who are going to give great contributions AND not slow you down or stifle your progression. To attract these individuals, you need to be that kind of collaborator. That means striving to get feedback to your collaborators in a timely manner. That is why, when a collaborator sends me a manuscript to review for upcoming submission, it becomes my top priority. Unless I have a pressing deadline (such as a grant proposal), these articles rise to the top of my to-do list the minute I get that email. If you have a collaborator who does not reply back to you in a timely manner, it's helpful to set a deadline with the collaborator by which you would like to submit the work. If the collaborator is taking an extreme amount of time, sometimes you may even need to move forward without their feedback.

Be Constructively Critical

Just as you wouldn't want to collaborate with people who constantly pat you on the back, you should strive to provide insightful feedback that will help create a better overall product. As you review the manuscripts, imagine you are a journal reviewer. Try to look ahead and foresee what problems a reviewer would find in the manuscript and then make your case to the author about why and how you think it could be addressed in advance of submission. Of course, nobody likes to just hear the negative. While you don't want to focus primarily on telling the author what is good about the manuscript, you should identify *specific* things you liked or were impressed with along the way and let them know. A comment like, "Good paper," at the end isn't nearly as meaningful as "Wow, I was especially impressed with the creative design of Study 2. Nicely done." Everybody likes receiving specific, positive feedback, and, if the person is sensitive, it can take the edge off the constructive criticism offered. If you can phrase criticism in a positive way, that also helps. For example, "I see what you were trying to do here, but reviewers might say X." Also, specific compliments tell the author more concretely what exactly was good about the paper so the author knows what to continue doing for future papers.

Provide Occasional Updates

It is good to keep your collaborators up to date on your joint projects. For instance, I have a few papers on which I was a coauthor that were submitted more than a year ago and I'm still wondering what happened to them. Although you may think it's embarrassing to get rejected, most seasoned scholars are used to rejection and won't think less of you because the paper was rejected. Instead, they are happy to find out what happened to the paper and to receive a forwarded rejection letter so they can know why it was rejected. If they never know if or why the manuscript was rejected then they don't know what to fix in future manuscripts. Basically, it's a waste of a valuable feedback.

It's also helpful to keep coauthors posted on manuscripts you are preparing for submission. Everyone is busy and people understand when things take longer than initially planned: that's just part of academia. However, it's nice to know that a particular paper is still on your radar. Letting coauthors know where you stand on the paper is an important part of accountability, which can help motivate you to make further progress. It also lets other collaborators know you didn't drop the ball. If they think you completely gave up on the project after all their hard work, then would they want to collaborate with you in the future? Probably not.

Express Gratitude

People who have taken the time to provide feedback and improve your manuscript deserve to be thanked. The more specific you can be about what you're grateful for, the better. A generic "thank you" doesn't go nearly as far as finding something very specific to thank the person for (e.g., "I really liked the idea you added regarding self-perception theory, that added a lot to the manuscript"). If the person's contribution did not merit authorship, consider thanking the person in the footnote on the first page of the manuscript and letting them know that you did so. A little bit of gratitude can go a long way to helping someone feel valued. It will also make them want to continue to work closely with you.

Chapter Summary

Good collaborators are probably the most important resource for productivity. Some important qualities to look for include productivity, proficiency in a certain skill, and a critical mind. Also, remember that to have great collaborators, you need to be a great collaborator. Respond quickly and with specific constructive comments. Providing updates on the status of manuscripts and expressing gratitude are a few other ways to demonstrate your value as a collaborator. The next section describes how you can protect yourself from productivity pitfalls.

Chapter 8 Wrap-Up Exercises

1. Write about one or two things you found most helpful in this chapter that you want to apply to your career.

Finding Good Colleagues

2. List three individuals that could be valuable collaborators (these may overlap with those you listed from the previous chapter):

   Person #1_____

   Person #2_____

   Person #3_____

3. Write about what collaborative qualities you see in person #1 and about your plan to initiate collaboration with person #1:
4. Write about what collaborative qualities you see in person #2 and about your plan to initiate collaboration with person #2:
5. Write about what collaborative qualities you see in person #3 and about your plan to initiate collaboration with person #3:

Becoming Everyone's Favorite Collaborator

6. Write about one or two things you could do to be a better collaborator in the future.

Part III
Pitfall Prevention

You have made it nearly halfway through the book and have learned about how to gain academic prosperity through the key elements of priorities and efficiency. I view priorities as the foundation, and without this you won't get much done, period. When you have the motivation and time that comes from proper prioritizing, you need to channel these well by enhancing your efficiency. I compare this efficiency to the walls of your home. However, a house is incomplete without a roof. If your structure has a solid foundation with great walls, your structure won't be worth much without a roof when the storms come. To prevent major damage, you'll need to be aware of the primary productivity pitfalls.

These pitfalls come in two types, both internal and external. In Chapter 9, I will discuss the five enemies from within and how the potentially devastating effects of each can be mitigated. Next, I describe burnout and how to conquer this internal dragon with a balanced lifestyle (Chapter 10). I then discuss how to deal with the pitfalls that come from without, including distractions (Chapter 11) and rejection (Chapter 12). Awareness of and strategies for dealing with the pitfalls that come from both within and without can help keep a warm, dry roof on your academic prosperity.

Once you have put up your preventative roofing material, your mansion is now complete. Here's what it looks like!

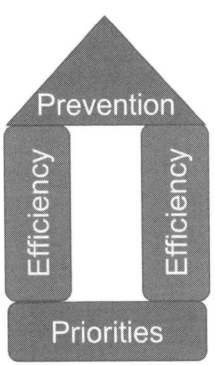

Figure 9.1 Principles of Enhanced Productivity

9   Avoid Five Enemies From Within

Main Chapter Points

- In high doses, perfectionism, procrastination, idealism, cynicism, and a know-it-all attitude can be very detrimental to productivity.
- Pulverize the procrastinator by following the suggestions in Part I for creating urgency.
- Put off perfectionism by waiting until later drafts to be perfectionistic, putting away your pride of thinking that many people are closely reading what you write, and putting down your guard through free writing.
- Inform the idealist that most people contribute through small, incremental findings.
- Sic the cynic by remembering that all research has flaws.
- Knock out the know-it-all by remembering the purpose of an introduction, by identifying when you are reading literature to procrastinate writing, and by reading to write.

Chapter Introduction

> Upon the close of their first year of graduate school, the department chair conversed with five frustrated faculty members about their new students. The chair concluded that each member of the incoming cohort of students seemed to have a major hang-up that limited their productivity.
>
> Tony, the first graduate student discussed, was very bright and had great intentions, but he just never seemed to get to his research. His advisor informed the chair that when Tony was given an assignment, he would come up with excuse after excuse when asked why it hadn't been completed. Every time they set a deadline, something always seemed to come up that prevented Tony from meeting the deadline.
>
> Sarah was a great writer and very polished. You would never see typos or errors in what she wrote; however, she had such high standards that she

didn't want anyone to see her work until it was perfect in her eyes. Her advisor pointed out that giving her any negative feedback set her back even further because the next time around, she was even more fastidious about each and every detail in the study. She seemed paralyzed by feedback, and her advisor didn't know what to do to help move things along.

Tim came into graduate school with a mission. He wanted to drastically change society for the better with his research. His advisor reported that when approached with an idea for a future study, Tim would usually turn it down because it didn't seem like the type of thing that would have a big impact on society. Finally, he began working on something, and the results actually panned out according to Tim's hypothesis. However, the effect of the results was rather weak. Tim seriously questioned whether it actually meant anything important and hadn't gotten around to writing anything up about it.

Steve was perhaps the brightest of the bunch and was on a university fellowship, so he wasn't even required to do research for his stipend. His advisor reported that Steve had learned a great deal about his chosen topic. In fact, it was impressive just how well he seemed to know the literature, as he spent a great deal of time reading everything he could find on his topic. Although Steve and his advisor had several great discussions about his topic, Steve hadn't gotten past writing a literature review during his first year.

Jessica really enjoyed the Introduction to Methods class because she felt like she was finally becoming a more informed consumer of research. She was naturally a critical thinker, but this class seemed to equip her with the knowledge of all the inherent flaws in every research design. She loved to tear apart studies and got outstanding grades on all of her critical review papers. The only problem was the methods used by her current advisor drew the same fire. Despite the advisor pointing out that every method has its limitations, Jessica was exhaustive in noting all the potential flaws in the studies they planned, and this had created a wedge between them. In fact, their mutual collaboration had come to a standstill.

Upon hearing these reports, the department chair was at a loss as to what should be done. The productivity of the entire department was being hampered by this cohort. *Well, there's always next year*, the chair thought to herself. But what she didn't know was that there are ways to fix each of these pitfalls.

Enemies lurk at every corner and would like nothing more than to knock you off the path of productivity. Unfortunately, many of these enemies come from within. Most of us probably have at least one of these foes we deal with from time to time, and being aware of them can help you fight them off. They include the procrastinator, the perfectionist, the idealist, the cynic, and the know-it-all. These five enemies all exude poisonous gas that can asphyxiate the publishing genius within you. I have seen each of these five foes attack and even debilitate people who have done so much work to receive a Ph.D., leaving them unproductive and jobless. Let's discuss each one and some solutions for dealing with them.

The Procrastinator

Probably the most pervasive of the five foes is the procrastinator. The sneaky thing about the procrastinator is that he can make you feel justified in your procrastination by engaging you with several urgent but less important tasks. For example, you may need to finish writing so you can get a manuscript submitted, but the procrastinator will tell you that you really ought to finish doing some grading, or finish writing the class assignment that's due next week. Thus, you end up feeling like you are on task and being productive while pushing back and procrastinating that which carries far more weight. If you continue to trade that which is urgent for that which is important, you'll get stuck accomplishing very little research during your career. To stop this enemy in its tracks we should pulverize it.

Pulverize the Procrastinator

Probably the best strategy for defeating the procrastinator is to apply the principles of putting first things first that we discussed in Chapter 2. These principles will really help you to heighten the urgency and importance of your research. If you are successful at enhancing the importance and especially the urgency of research in your life, the tendency for procrastination will be diminished. For instance, force yourself to do the more difficult, but important, tasks first. Many successful scholars schedule research or writing time into their daily schedule, making procrastination less likely.

Being excited about your research topic (see Chapter 3) is also important, because if you enjoy doing it, you will be less likely to procrastinate spending time on it. You may consider making the research tasks more appealing by offering yourself incentives for reaching certain milestones as well as celebrating your achievements.

The Perfectionist

The second enemy that hampers the productivity of many scholars is the trap of perfectionism. Some people believe everything should be absolutely perfect before submitting a paper for publication or even to collaborators. Unfortunately, for many graduate students some professors are this way, making it nearly impossible to get something out the door in a reasonable period of time. Also, when a perfectionist has their error in thinking or in writing exposed by a collaborator or reviewer, they often take it personally and may become even more reluctant to send it out for review. This can be very devastating for many researchers. Although a final draft of a manuscript should be free of typos and well-written, don't let the desire to achieve perfection prevent you from submitting manuscripts in a timely manner.

On perfectionism, Elbow (1973) advised,

> Fear of badness is probably what holds people back from developing power in writing. If you care too much about avoiding bad writing, you will be too cautious, too afraid to relinquish control. Whereas if you go all out for excellence and don't worry about the bad writing that comes with it, before long you will be able to produce writing that people will really want to read—even to buy. (p. 31)

To progress as a researcher and writer, you've got to relinquish control. You need to put off the perfectionist within you.

Put Off the Perfectionist

There are three ways to "put off" perfectionism. Even though I just discussed the problems with procrastination, it can be a useful tool in helping to combat perfectionism. Putting off pride and putting down your guard are also important ways of putting off perfectionism.

Procrastinate perfectionism. One of the best ways to stop the perfectionist is by temporarily unleashing the procrastinator on the perfectionist. You could tell yourself, "I'll wait until later to get it to that level." Of course you want your manuscript to be very polished when you submit it, but remind yourself that this is partly why we have reviewers—to help make a good manuscript better. If you keep putting off your desire for perfection until after the copyeditor has gone through it, there will be little extra work left for you to do. Remember this is the job of reviewers, editors, and copyeditors: to help you improve your work. If you insist on perfection at every stage, you are not letting these individuals do their fair share of the work.

Put off your pride. I believe pride and worrying about what others think of you is often at the heart of perfectionism. Part of this pride tells you that many people are going to be reading every word of what you have written. This is what adolescent researchers call an "imaginary audience." This refers to a state in which you imagine and believe that multitudes of people are listening to or following you at all times, for good or for ill. It is common during adolescence, but unfortunately for most everyone, it may carry on to some degree throughout adulthood.

The sobering truth of the matter is there may be only a handful of people that read your article from start to finish and they will be comprised mostly of blind reviewers (assuming reviewers actually read everything, which they often do not) and some students. Productive scholars are too busy with their own writing to read much more than your abstract. In fact, the only thing you should really be perfectionistic about is your title, since most readers won't get beyond that. There aren't people out there keeping tallies about how good of a writer you are or keeping close tabs on the actual content of your articles; rather, other scholars are far too busy worrying about themselves. Your research and writing ought to be good enough to convince the editor and reviewers, but believe me when I say there isn't an auditorium full of people who are critiquing what you've written. This may be somewhat disheartening, but it can also be quite liberating when you realize that most of what you write during your career will be read "cover-to-cover" by only a few people. With this in mind, perfectionism is nothing more than a waste of precious time.

Put down your guard. Ralph Waldo Emerson once said, "Do not be too timid and squeamish about your actions. All life is an experiment. The more experiments you make, the better." This is true for writing; sometimes you simply need to push yourself forward and experiment a bit. There's a common saying, "Write drunk, edit sober." Granted, I definitely don't promote getting drunk (especially while writing), but the idea is that being too uptight while you are writing an initial draft can stifle your writing and make it difficult to be as productive as you would be otherwise.

Martin (2011) suggested that, as researchers, we spend so much of our time criticizing the work of others that when we begin to write ourselves, it's very easy to be similarly critical: "Trouble arises, though, when this critical capacity is turned on when you try to write. The text simply doesn't measure up. The mind cries out in pain, 'It's no good! Change it! Delete!'" (p. 17). It's important to turn off that critical part in each of us as we write.

One way to turn off the critical part in us is through free writing. Many productivity coaches (e.g., Elbow, 1973) advocate free writing, or writing whatever occurs to you in a stream of consciousness without censoring or stopping. Such writing generates momentum and can help the perfectionist to get some ideas down in a much quicker manner without the self-censoring that slows you down. You can just write "(citation)" instead of going to find a reference as you are free writing and then go back and find the reference later. Similarly, you can go back later on and fix and improve what you have written, but many find they can make much better progress by getting the ideas out quickly. Just get it written and then perfect it later on.

The Idealist

The idealist wants to change the world. This is a healthy, good desire to have. However, those idealists out there should not expect to drastically change the world through their research. A researcher's job is to examine and describe phenomena, and unfortunately the typical work of most researchers is not groundbreaking. Scientists most often make small, incremental advances in knowledge, but the idealist is not satisfied with such advances. An idealist is bored by such findings and has the attitude of "The effect size is so small—why does it even matter to real people? How is this miniscule finding going to change lives? This significant finding isn't even worth writing up."

In writing about what prevents scholars from writing, Boice (1997) suggests that less productive writers "suppose that writing must be novel, substantial, and unforced. And they repeatedly claim that most of what gets published falls far below their own standards" (p. 20). Idealists only want to spend time writing groundbreaking research and thus they don't write much of anything at all. How can the idealist enemy in each of us be overcome?

Inform the Idealist

The idealist is difficult to overcome but could be informed by looking around at your field and others and noting the lack of real monumental change. For instance, if you begin following politics closely and see the amount of deadlock and the inefficiencies and ineffectiveness of government programs, you begin to realize it isn't just science that has problems. Even though monumental change is difficult to note in this field or others, change *does* happen because of the work we do. I encourage the idealist to look for the small ways in which research in their field (especially using the examples of colleagues) has made a difference, thus learning to be satisfied with small but still positive change.

The Cynic

Most graduate methods classes teach students the ins and outs of research and how to be critical. A transformation takes place during this first year of graduate school from being a naïve consumer of research and believing everything you read to recognizing the flaws in every study and becoming skeptical. This can be healthy in several ways, but some take it to the extreme and tend to reject nearly all research because of inherent limitations. The cynic becomes critical of the field and skeptical of other researchers' trustworthiness. In fact, the cynic will also likely see problems with her own research design and methods and wonder if it's actually worth the bother to write something that is so inherently flawed. I actually once knew someone who was both an idealist and a cynic. Needless to say, he didn't make it very long before dropping out of the field. We need to sic the cynic within.

Sic the Cynic

It is important to realize that all research has flaws, but these flaws are largely attributable to natural limitations of measurement. The hard sciences seem to have it easier regarding these issues, but dealing with human subjects is inherently messy and imprecise. Humans are complicated and the study of them is as complex as it is fuzzy. Yet, it's still worth the try, and the field in general has become more methodologically advanced over the years. You can make your field better from within if you don't become cynical and give up on it.

The Know-it-all

There are two types of professors: the producers of research and the consumers of research. I'm aware of professors in prominent positions who spend the majority of their time reading, synthesizing, and criticizing what others have done. It's a lot easier to sit on the sidelines criticizing the work of others than it is to produce something worthwhile yourself. In fact, endless literature reviewing can be a way of procrastinating actually doing the work yourself. Some may rationalize that they need to become an expert and read everything that was done in on a topic before they can begin to write and publish in that area. Of course, it is important to do an adequate search of the literature—reviewers will be annoyed if you haven't looked closely enough to have cited their key articles—but there comes a point where you need to just write and submit. Three suggestions will help you to knock out the know-it-all.

Knock Out the Know-it-all

Don't let the desire to become a know-it-all get in the way of being a productive writer. You can knock out the know-it-all by remembering the purpose of an introduction, by identifying when you are reading literature to procrastinate writing, and by reading to write.

Remember the purpose of an introduction. As mentioned in Chapter 5, many people mistakenly think the purpose of an introduction is to bore the reader by shoving everything that has been written on a particular topic down their throat. This is not the case at all, and it takes much more time and effort to do it the wrong way than it does to do it the right way. The purpose of a good introduction is not to thoroughly review all that has been done on your topic, but to derive your hypotheses. You simply need to give the reader enough background to support the specific hypothesis you are testing in the study, end of story. When you try to show off all you know by giving the reader the kitchen-sink type of introduction, you don't impress; rather, you confuse the reader because it becomes difficult for her to decipher exactly what the purpose of the manuscript is. So, save yourself a great deal of time and save the reader a great deal of confusion by reviewing only the literature that is relevant to your hypothesis.

Purposeful preparation versus procrastinative preparation. Okay, so I admit that I made up a new word, "Procrastinative," but I think it works to describe the type of preparation that goes above and beyond what is actually needed for a research article. When it comes down to it, we can actually use reviewing the literature as a way to procrastinate writing. O'Hanlon (2007) suggests that many people spend a lot of time "preparing" as a way to procrastinate or avoid actually writing. He encourages writers to take an honest look at their time in preparation and planning and determine what is necessary and what is really procrastination in disguise.

It can be easy to deceive yourself that you are being productive when you spend a great deal of time preparing to write. Some of this is justified, but you've got to learn to recognize when you've crossed the threshold of purposeful preparation into procrastinative preparation. One extremely useful technique for avoiding procrastinative preparation is reading to write.

Read to write. Perhaps the best cure for the tendency to spend too much time reading the literature is to flip your previously held strategy on its head. Boice (1997) suggests that most scholars read to learn. This is actually not an effective strategy if you want to be a productive writer. Instead, read to write, or read to fill in the holes of an already drafted paper. Instead of letting the know-it-all take over and insist that you go through every ounce of the literature and write up a bulky literature review, Boice recommends that you do a great deal of prewriting. Just write out much of your article, perhaps during free writing, and then go back and fill in the blanks with citations. That way you are including that which is most relevant to your hypothesis, and you aren't tempted to include something simply because you already put so much time and effort into reading and summarizing the article. This will focus your search of the literature so that you can quickly find exactly what you need to back up a certain point that you have already written about. Better yet, if you are working with students, have them look up and add the references for you, then check to ensure their work is accurate.

I try to spend as little time reviewing literature as I can. I would rather delegate as much of that tedious work as I can to others and spend most of my time writing. I'm inclined to believe that the most productive scholars share this style; it's just not possible to be a prolific researcher if you spend most of your time reading to learn rather than reading to write.

Chapter Summary

In low doses, perfectionism, procrastination, idealism, cynicism, and a know-it-all attitude can be healthy and will promote good scholarship. However, any of these can quickly become viral and weaken your ability to be productive if not contained. The key is to turn these five enemies into assets by using each in moderation. Burnout is another enemy from within, but its complexity requires an entirely separate chapter, which I will address next.

Chapter 9 Wrap-Up Exercises

1. Write about one or two things you found most helpful in this chapter that you want to apply to your career.
2. We all have a tendency toward one or more of these five enemies from within. Based on what you've read, which one(s) poses the most danger for you personally? Why?
3. What specific precautions might you take to reduce the potential impact of this foe?

10 Feed the Flame
Avoid Burnout

Main Chapter Points

- Sharpen your saw by maintaining a healthy balance in the areas of physical health, intellectual stimulation, self-introspection, and social interaction.
- Find fun, validation, and motivation by attending conferences frequently.
- Celebrate your victories to fan the flames of future achievement.

Chapter Introduction

> Samantha was a workaholic. She was so engaged with her academic career that it consumed all of her time. She no longer found the time to exercise, ate mostly fast food, didn't get enough sleep, and didn't have time left over for her friends and family. When the people in life complained about being starved for time with her, she would point out that the tenure clock was ticking and if she didn't publish, her career would perish. She'd heard about others that didn't make tenure and she wasn't going to let it happen to her. Yet, even though she was spending more time than ever working, her overall productivity hadn't substantially risen, which caused her to be frustrated and want to work even harder. She blamed the insufficient increase in productivity on her health; she got sick more often than usual and this really slowed her down. Even when she was fully healthy, she noticed her mind wandering and she wasn't able to stay focused as long as she used to. If she was frankly honest with herself, she wasn't even enjoying all the time she spent on research like she did in the past, and she was starting to wonder whether she'd be able to maintain this pace. These thoughts left her in despair, because with tenure review around the corner, she simply couldn't afford to get burned out. What could she do?

To this point we have discussed some very important keys which, if applied consistently, could dramatically boost your research productivity and career success. However, if you are unable to sustain motivation and avoid burnout, like Samantha, these principles will not have a lasting benefit for you. In this chapter, I discuss three strategies for feeding the flame of your productivity engine so you can sustain high levels of productivity throughout your career while maintaining a happy, healthy life. These include living a balanced life by making goals for other important areas such as physical health, intellectual stimulation, self-introspection, and social interaction. I also discuss how frequent academic conference attendance and celebrating your achievements can provide additional fuel to help keep that productivity fire burning brightly.

Live a Balanced Life: Sharpening the Saw

In his book, *Seven Habits of Highly Effective People*, Covey (1989) discusses the concept of "sharpening the saw." Essentially, after repeated use and without proper care, a saw will inevitably become dull and is no longer as effective at performing its job. Can you imagine trying to hack down a tree with a dull saw? Not so effective. In essence, it would undo everything this book has tried to help develop! Not understanding that their blade has become dull, some people increase their effort, sawing and hacking away, thinking if they just push harder, they will see the same results they had received previously. Given the analogy of sawing a tree down, this is obviously flawed thinking; the solution is clearly to take a break from the work of sawing and sharpen the saw. That is why despite Samantha's increase in effort and time, her productivity was not enhanced.

Many feel guilty for taking time off to live a balanced life. We often think of the time we will lose in sawing if we stop to sharpen the saw. However, this time is well worth any perceived loss in productivity, because a sharpened saw will be much more effective at performing its job and will do it in less time. In the field of academia, sometimes it's easy to get carried away with the excitement of research and publishing and neglect some of the other areas of life that are just as essential in helping you to continue to perform at a high level of effectiveness. If you become unbalanced, your saw will inevitably become dull and you will lose steam and burn out.

Life has much more to offer than success at work. I like to keep in mind four primary domains and actually set goals in each domain to help keep my life in balance. These four domains are physical health, intellectual stimulation, self-introspection, and social interaction, all of which require considerable effort but are very important for keeping your saw sharpened. I try to pair activities from different categories together to maximize efficiency; however, this may not match your style. I provide some ideas that have worked for me, but I encourage you to consider your preferences and values and decide what would best help you to keep your life in balance.

Physical Health

Physical health is a core part of life. Let's face it: researchers typically lead rather sedentary lives. We aren't running around nailing boards down, mowing lawns, or doing any heavy lifting. It can be very easy to slip into physical inactivity, especially when you are stressed about graduate school or about getting tenure. Yet putting off adequate physical exercise will catch up to you both in the short term and in the long run. In the short term, physical exercise is always worth the time that it takes because it helps relieve stress (for a review, see Salmon, 2001) and allows your mind to more effectively process information. In the long run, keeping your body in shape will extend your life and the time you have to pursue your career goals. Here are some ideas for adding exercise and healthy eating to an already busy schedule.

1. **Commuting by bike.** I live not far from campus, and the region where I live is extremely hilly, so it's a good workout. There have been several occasions where I have left home at the same exact time as some of the friends in my neighborhood who drive and have beaten them to campus. You may be able to guess why: parking is atrocious at most universities. As these friends are finding a place to park and walking from the lot to the building, I pass them up and conveniently park my bike right in front of my building. Not only does this provide me with nearly an hour of exercise every day, but it has negated the need for my family to buy a second vehicle, saving us a great deal of money in monthly payments, insurance, and gas. I also don't have to set aside any extra time for it, which is one of the main reasons individuals don't work out.
2. **Utilize your university's resources.** I am unaware of the policies at all universities, yet the one I attended required all students pay a gym fee regardless of whether or not they utilized it. Surely, you are paying for the gym whether directly or indirectly. It could be that you have been paying all this time for other people to get in great shape! If the gym is not free, students and faculty members usually get a bargain deal for state-of-the-art facilities. Lifting weights not only relieves stress and burns calories as you lift, but the muscles you build boost your metabolism and burn more calories when you are in a state of rest. Your university will likely have a pool, and swimming is great for getting a full body workout and can be an especially useful form of exercise if you have any joint problems.

    The great thing about working out at your university's facilities is it's more time efficient. You could fit in a workout right before work, right after work, or, my personal favorite, right in the middle of work to give your mind a break. Just think, there's a good chance you are paying for others to be healthy, so why not get your money's worth and join in the fun? If you struggle with motivation, consider finding another student or faculty member who would like to be your gym buddy. Having a gym buddy is a good way to hold yourself accountable, stay motivated, and

even socialize. You also may consider purchasing some inexpensive equipment and exercising at home. This could be a nice way to watch your favorite TV show while getting your daily workout.
3. **Pack a lunch.** Most graduate students and new professionals go out for lunch every day. Not only does this cost a great deal (if you are in this habit, I challenge you to keep a close record for a week or month to see how much you are actually spending on food), but it's also extremely unhealthy. An equally dangerous and common approach is to purchase microwaveable frozen meals that are typically very high in sodium, fat, and calories. Instead, consider packing a lunch. If you don't have time to cook (which is true for most of us), you could consider putting together a sandwich on whole wheat bread (which takes no more than 3–4 minutes) or making larger portions when you do cook so you have plenty left over for future meals. As an undergraduate, I would cook a huge pot of spaghetti every Sunday that I would eat from for the whole week. Fruits and vegetables are another option that are often forgotten but can be quick and easy to pack and contain vitamins and nutrients essential for good health.
4. **Get enough sleep.** Sometimes it may feel like you can't afford to sleep. However, when you deprive yourself of sleep for too long you begin to be less effective during the day. You will not feel your best and the time lost as a result would be much better spent in bed. You may be able to caffeinate yourself to bring you up to speed when you need it, but it will eventually catch up to you and hurt your overall productivity. Doctors recommend between 7–8 hours.

Making these small changes in your lifestyle will make a world of difference in both your health and your pocketbook. Remember that to be truly healthy (and thereby a much more effective researcher), you have to wage a multi-front war. It's not enough just to exercise; you must also be careful about the type and quantity of calories you are consuming and how much sleep you are getting.

Outside Intellectual Stimulation

Naturally, as researchers, we use our minds a great deal and are provided with all kinds of opportunities for mental stimulation. However, to be well balanced, it is not enough to engage in your own research or to simply keep up on the research in your field. As scholars, we shouldn't live in a box. Here are a few ideas for obtaining balance with mental goals.

1. **Read a broad range of materials.** You may be thinking that you don't even have the time to adequately keep up on the findings in your own field, let alone read more broadly. I have often felt the same way. So how can this be accomplished? Audiobooks! I don't read physical books very often; however, I usually get through 2–3 books each month. If you

replied, "But audio books are incredibly expensive," you would be right on the money, unless you check them out from your local library. You can also get many audio books online that are public domain legally and free, such as LibriVox. Your local library has an increasing selection of classic books you could listen to in the car during your commute or download onto an MP3 player to listen to as you exercise or clean. iPads or E-Readers are also great sources to enable you to take advantage of waiting time to stimulate yourself intellectually.

2. **Stay current on current events.** This may not be a priority for you at this point in your life, but I think it's important to be at least somewhat informed about what is going on in the world—it's part of being a responsible citizen. Whether it be browsing headlines on the Internet, listening to a news broadcast in the car or on the TV at home while exercising, or by reading the newspaper during breakfast, you'll be a better professional if you can be at least somewhat conversant about what is going on in the world. It may even spark new research ideas!

Self-Introspection

Being in touch with who you are and where you are going in life can enhance your personal happiness and peace, as well as provide needed insight as to how best to sharpen your saw. According to Socrates, "The unexamined life is not worth living." I take this to mean that if you are never thinking introspectively about your life and the direction you are going, your life will not be everything it could be. What are some ways you can stay in touch with your spiritual side? You may consider going out in nature, writing your thoughts down in a journal, meditating, or doing some other activity that helps you to engage in introspection.

Social Interaction

As I pointed out in previous chapters, strong professional relationships are vital to research productivity. However, other non-professional social relationships are also very important for productivity as they provide emotional support and revive us in many ways. Yet, from my observations, the social networks of many academics do not extend far beyond the people in their field. Although these relationships can extend beyond academic production, always hanging out with people that are doing things that you do can limit you from enriching conversations that could broaden your perspective. Here are a few ideas for broadening your social network.

1. **Join a volunteer organization.** A great way to associate with high-caliber people who can enrich your life is to join a volunteer organization. I've noticed that some of the best people to associate with are those who want to serve others. There are so many options in every community depending on your interests. If you care about nature, you could volunteer with local

parks and recreation. If you are concerned about children, you could join the Parent Teacher Organization or a Children's Advocacy Group. If you are religiously inclined, many local churches regularly perform volunteer services you could become involved in. If you feel it is important to help those in need, you could volunteer at a shelter.

You are not only socially enriched by interacting with those you serve, but can build strong, lasting relationships with those you serve *with*. The majority of my most meaningful relationships have been formed while serving others in the volunteer organization I am involved with. I have noticed that the social networks of many of my graduate school colleagues are comprised mostly of fellow graduate students. Having the association of others in a diverse volunteer group can be very enriching because I learned a lot about different fields or work and different perspectives.

Also, if you are reading this book, it likely indicates that you have been blessed with many great opportunities. Give back through serving others. The irony is that the more you attempt to give back by serving, the more your life will be blessed and enriched.

2. **Develop your talents with others.** Aside from your obvious intellectual gifts, we all have other talents or interests that can enrich our lives. Whether it is in music, athletics, art, public speaking, or something else, further developing these talents can be a socially enriching experience. Join a local choir or soccer club, take art classes, or sign up for your local Toastmasters club (public speaking group). Not only will you find it exhilarating to discover and develop your talents, but the relationships you can form along the way could prove to be life-changing.

3. **Remember that loved ones spell love T-I-M-E.** Whatever stage of life we are in, we all have especially close relationships, whether with parents, siblings, a romantic partner, or children. Just as garden plants will wither and die without water, these close relationships can be adversely affected if they aren't given enough quality time. Let loved ones into your life, share your experiences with them, and listen carefully as they share theirs. Being a good listener takes time and effort, but I believe it to be one of the greatest ways to communicate love and concern. More than likely, these family relationships will be long-lasting, and it will be these people who attend your funeral. I've heard it said no one on their deathbed ever wishes they had spent more time in the office. Instead, regrets typically center on not spending time with those who matter most to us, and the best way to let them know they matter is by giving them your time.

Overworking will provide diminishing returns so your "saw" will eventually become dull and you will burn out. Ironically, the best way to ensure continued productivity is to spend sufficient time developing yourself physically, intellectually, self-introspectively, and socially. I'm definitely not advocating that you shouldn't work very hard, because that is probably the most crucial element for productivity. However, if you efficiently make the most of every minute of every day, while working to keep your life in balance, you can be a productive researcher and still have a life. Although it may seem overwhelming to develop yourself in all four of these areas while still producing excellent research, there are many activities that essentially kill two birds with one stone. For example, you may go to a museum or art exhibit with friends or family. You can also go on a short camping trip or a leisurely bike ride with loved ones. All of these activities can enrich your life in multiple domains. Of course, too much time in any of these domains can throw your life out of balance and be detrimental. Finding and maintaining this balance in life may be the most fascinating quest of your life.

Attend Academic Conferences Frequently

One of the biggest perks of academia is the opportunity to attend conferences in various cities throughout your nation and the world. Attendance can feed your fire in multiple ways. It allows you the chance to travel and see new things and the chance to be validated by and plan studies with people that are interested in your research.

1. **Subsidized travel opportunity.** Not everyone enjoys traveling, but if you do, conferences are an amazing way to often have at least a portion of your travel expenses covered by your university. If my conference is domestic, I will arrange my flights to arrive a day early or to stay a day after the conference ends so I can spend at least half a day touring the conference city (which in my field is almost always somewhere fun and different each year). Whether it was roaming down the river walk in San Antonio, eating a shrimp sandwich at Fisherman's Wharf in San Francisco, or soaring on an airboat through the Everglades outside of Fort Meyers, I have found the experience to be enriching and rejuvenating. Of course, be ethical and pay out of pocket for any non-conference related expenses. Also, don't go to a conference just for the location; it should be pertinent to the advancement of your career.

    If traveling internationally, I stay for much longer. For example, last summer I attended a conference in Tel Aviv, Israel. Before the conference began, I visited Egypt and Turkey, and after the conference, I took a bus tour of Israel. Of course, I was not reimbursed for any of my touring expenses; however, the flight to the Middle East was by far the biggest expense of my trip, and I viewed this as a once-in-a-lifetime experience. Getting the opportunity to see exotic cities and to experience new cultures can give you something to look forward to as you sit behind your computer all day. It breaks up the monotony and can even help you to come up with research ideas for the future.

2. **Validation from other researchers.** Perhaps this may be different for you, but in my particular field, we often scientifically prove phenomena

that the layperson thinks may be obvious or just "no big deal." Because of this, validation can be hard to find from the average person. I'll never forget on Christmas Eve one year, I was excitedly telling a large group of friends and family about my research findings when my sister-in-law piped up and asked, "Don't we already know that?" I was humiliated! After that and other similar experiences during the holiday break, I hit the biggest motivation slump of my life that took nearly three weeks to pull out of. Unfortunately, this wasn't an isolated incident, as this has often been my experience when I discuss my research with people outside my field who don't really understand all that goes into a study.

Conversely, every time you attend a conference, it's like entering some kind of magical make-believe world in which you are surrounded by other people who share your enthusiasm for researching in your field. You will likely even find people who are passionate about your specific area of expertise. Being able to share with others what I've been doing and finding out about their research legitimizes and validates what I spend my time doing each day. I find that my motivation is highest right after a conference, and I honestly believe a lot of it has to do with the validation that comes from talking to others who are a part of my world.

3. **Setting concrete plans into action.** Another motivating aspect of a conference is the opportunity to meet up with collaborators and make specific plans for conducting or writing up your research. It always seems to be more effective to meet and discuss plans in person, so creating this opportunity through conference attendance will be extremely helpful. When you come home, you will likely have specific projects to work on based on the connections you made at the conference, and this can help enhance your motivation and prevent burnout.

In sum, frequently attending conferences can safeguard you from losing motivation and burning out by providing you an opportunity to break up your regular routine and to travel to an exciting destination. Conferences also afford you with a chance to have your research validated and to make concrete plans for future work.

Celebrate Your Victories

I recently had a respected colleague of mine tell me that he regrets not stopping to celebrate his milestones of achievement. I'm hoping not to make that mistake. To give you an example of this, as I'm writing this chapter, I am sitting 30 feet from the waves crashing on the beach in Puerto Rico. The reason for this trip? I just accepted an offer for a job, and my wife and I are celebrating by taking a well-deserved vacation! We spent a pleasurable day walking around old San Juan and enjoying the breathtaking views from atop 17th-century forts, and we made plans for tomorrow to hike in the rainforest and enjoy the beach. It was honestly one of the happiest days of my life.

When you celebrate your achievements, it is like waving a large carrot in front of your subconscious, which can then help push you on to even greater heights of accomplishment. I have another colleague who goes out to dinner with his wife each time he gets a publication. Whatever you deem to be a good reward, take it and savor the moment. Make it a poignantly pleasant experience and you will keep yourself excited to reach your next milestone.

Chapter Summary

Without having a plan to maintain and "feed your fire" of productivity, all the other keys in this book will come to naught. Sharpen your saw by maintaining a healthy balance in the areas of physical health, intellectual stimulation, self-introspection, and social interaction. Find fun, validation, and motivation by attending conferences frequently. Finally, fan the flames of future achievement by thoroughly celebrating your victories.

We've now covered several primary enemies from within, which are dangerous to be sure. However, the enemies from without can be even more malicious. For example, the next enemy to our productivity can infiltrate our computers, our phones, and our offices.

Chapter 10 Wrap-Up Exercises

1. Write about one or two things you found most helpful in this chapter that you want to apply to your career.
2. Maintaining balance in other aspects of life is crucial to your long-term professional success. Write down three goals you have for each of the four domains.

Physical Health

Goal #1_____

Goal #2_____

Goal #3_____

Intellectual Stimulation

Goal #1_____

Goal #2_____

Goal #3_____

Self-Introspection

Goal #1 _____

Goal #2 _____

Goal #3 _____

Social Interaction

Goal #1 _____

Goal #2 _____

Goal #3 _____

3. Next, write about the next conference you plan to attend as well as any potential collaborators with whom you could plan a study.
4. Write about an achievement you anticipate in the near future and your plan to celebrate and reward yourself for that achievement.

11 Diminish Distractions

Main Chapter Points

- Distractions can prevent and interrupt flow and diminish your ability to complete a task effectively.
- Technology distractions can be relegated to breaks and function as a reward for focused effort.
- Distractions from colleagues and students can be minimized with communication and planning.

Chapter Introduction

Paul has been waiting for Friday all week. This is the day when he doesn't have any classes or any other obligations, a day he can devote solely to writing and research. Paul sits down at his computer at about 8:00 a.m. Before beginning, however, Paul enjoys reading a few articles about some of his favorite topics—sports and politics. It is fall and college football is just beginning, making this an enticing topic. As a result Paul spends a bit more time reading articles about how his team played last Saturday as well as articles that size up the opponent for tomorrow's game. He's so excited, he can barely wait and it's hard to stop reading. All this competition makes him wonder about how the pundits reacted to the presidential debate the previous night. Did his candidate prevail? Paul gets caught up in another round of online article reading. It's now almost 10 a.m. 'Okay, Okay,' he tells himself, 'It's time to get going, but I better check my email to see if I've heard back from any of my collaborators.'

Paul has over a dozen emails in his inbox. One of them reminds him of a committee assignment he hasn't yet completed so he works on that for a while. Another email displays a bill he thinks he was overcharged for, so he calls customer service and battles that out. Another hour passes. One of the last emails alerts him that Suzie has commented on his Facebook

> status—how exciting. Once logged into Facebook, Paul sees that he has five new messages and four new friend requests. He replies to each of those and checks out some of the pictures of the people who are requesting his friendship, trying to try to remember how he knows them. He also sees some interesting updates from some of his friends and makes a few comments. Another hour passes; it is now noon and Paul's colleague Dennis stops by to see if he'd like to go out for some lunch. Dennis likes to go to nice, sit-down restaurants and so it's nearly 2 p.m. by the time they come back. This pattern continued and during his day of research, he only managed to write one new paragraph and partially revise another paragraph. 'Oh well, there's always next Friday,' Paul thinks to himself.

Perhaps you've had a day like Paul in which you had great intentions for getting a lot done, but your biggest achievement was replying to the emails of the day. This may be an extreme example, but I'm ashamed to admit that I've had days that mirror many aspects of Paul's day. In fact, people experience this loss of time much more than they realize. Many of us think we're getting a lot done, when in reality we aren't. Incredibly, 55% of faculty members who were asked, "Is this the busiest year of your life?" replied "yes" (Boice, 1989, p. 606). It's worth repeating the other element of this study as described in Chapter 1. These faculty members were asked to estimate how many hours they were working each week, and they claimed they were working 60 hours a week and spending 30 of those hours doing research. However, when they had to keep close records of how much time they actually spent by reporting their activities every 15 minutes, the reality was they had only worked an average of 29 hours per week, spending 90 minutes on research and only 30 minutes writing (Boice, 1989, p. 606). Wow! What a tragedy. I believe giving into distractions is a prime reason for the difference between perceived work and actual work.

This study by Boice was conducted in the 1980s, long before the modern era of distractions. The numbers may be even worse in our day with email, texting, tweeting, and chatting. I would even go so far as to argue that never before in history have individuals been confronted with more distractions than we have today, and it's becoming increasingly worse.

My mom is a gifted pianist and she wanted to pass that on to her children. She required us to practice for hours a day and would exact punishments, such as withholding money or grounding, to ensure that we practiced. Oftentimes my friends would be out playing and having a great time outside when I was stuck with Beethoven in the stuffy music room. In fact, one summer I was practicing the piano for four hours a day. When I balked at having to practice so much, she assured me that one day I would thank her.

I'm thanking you now, Mom, but not because I really use this talent very often—in fact I rarely play now. I thank my mom because all those hours sitting at that piano bench, day in and day out, taught me how to stay focused on a task for long periods of time. As a researcher, this is probably one of the most valuable skills you can cultivate toward becoming a productive scholar. If you don't yet have the skill of being able to focus on a project for several consecutive hours, know that it is not something you will be able to develop overnight. However, with a great deal of practice and self-control, there is a definite hope of improvement. Here are a few concepts to keep in mind about why being distracted can hamper you.

Flow

Have you ever had an experience where you started doing something and then came to yourself and realized you had just spent hours on that task and didn't even realize it? That's flow. Groundbreaking research done by Mihály Csíkszentmihályi (1998) described this state of being in which the mind is fully immersed and fully involved, a process called "flow." It is a completely focused motivation and a single-minded immersion on a task that stretches you just enough to keep you engaged without making you want to give up. During flow, emotions are channeled, energized, and completely aligned with the task at hand. When people enter a state of flow, it's almost like becoming superhuman in your strength and ability. When you are in a state of flow you can get so much more done than you normally are able to do. This is focused energy at its best.

You can probably recall experiencing flow and can recognize just how productive you were when you reached that state. I personally have reached this state a number of times while writing this book. It's amazing to see that I can write 12–15 pages in one sitting while at other times I will only write 2–3 pages in the same amount of time without flow.

It goes without saying how damaging distractions are to flow. Not only do distractions prevent you from getting into a state of flow, but they can quickly take you out of this state you worked so hard to attain.

Multitasking While Writing

I'm a firm believer in multitasking and I do it constantly. However, in light of recent research on this topic, I have reduced the amount of multitasking I engage in while doing research tasks. I'm still a big fan of multitasking in general, but I'm convinced there are many tasks where multitasking is inappropriate because they require your full attention. This includes many research tasks, especially writing. Studies indicate that we don't actually do a lot of things simultaneously; rather, we are able to switch our attention from one task to the next very quickly. "People can't multitask very well, and when people say they can, they're deluding themselves," said Dr. Earl Miller, a neuroscientist. "The brain is very good at deluding itself" (Hamilton, 2008, p. 1). This is particularly the case when the task involves both communicating via speech and by written word (Hamilton, 2008). Thus, we deceive ourselves when we think we can write or perform research while simultaneously engaging in some other form of media. With our attention diverted, we are not able to complete either task as well or as quickly as we could if we gave each one our undivided attention at separate times. Ultimately, trying to focus on two tasks will slow you down, not to mention it will disrupt any chance you have of entering into a state of superhuman productivity present during flow.

Though I have not yet fully mastered the art of not getting distracted, I *have* learned a few tricks I follow in order to minimize the distractions while I do research and writing. The following is a list of distractions that can hamper our productivity and then we'll discuss some general strategies for blocking out distractions.

Technology Distractions

I don't want to sound like I'm anti-technology, because I'm not. I think much can be gained from technological advances, and technology greatly enhances our capacity to be productive. I'm simply against these technological advances bombarding our focus and wreaking havoc on individual productivity. In a recent *New York Times* article (Ritchel, 2010) a girl admitted to sending 27,000 text messages in one month, 900 a day. If it takes half a minute to send a text message, and you multiply that by 900, then you can see that she could be spending approximately 7.5 hours per day just on text messaging. Unfortunately, sending hundreds of text messages is not as efficient as you may think.

Texting. This technology can be a fantastic way to communicate; however, it also seems to have great potential to divert attention. In fact, there are certain people with which you can't even have a 10-minute conversation without being interrupted by them texting someone else in the middle of it. Texting has become so pervasive in our society that I've been told that many people go out with friends, sit together, and all simultaneously text other people, so much so that people who aren't texting actually feel left out. It seems so ironic that we've gotten to the point where you can be with friends and feel left out for being the only one who isn't communicating with someone outside the group while you're together. Part of the problem with texting is that people have come to desire and even to expect instantaneous responses. When you reply to a text, your productivity is hampered or even immobilized as you are left wondering how the person will reply. Frequent texting can immobilize your concentration and ability to get into peak performance.

Email/Social Media. Let's face it, sitting behind a computer much of the day writing and researching can be a bit lonesome at times. Also, I think many of us do the majority of our communicating with others through email. That is why email can be such a welcome diversion—somebody was thinking of you! Unfortunately, email and social media like Facebook can become a huge time eater by themselves, but I think that an even bigger problem is that they interrupt the flow and focus of writing and research. Such messages and communication can drastically change our emotions, perhaps making us very excited about something (and thus drawing thoughts to that topic), worried, or angry, etc. This influx of emotion can really affect one's ability to write and focus. I've had nearly an entire day's productivity thrown off by seeing an email alert me of getting an unexpected $35 charge in my bank account. That news was so upsetting to me that it took a variety of other activities to return me to a state where I could write again. Additionally, if you are constantly flipping back and forth between checking emails and working, you won't be able to get nearly as much done.

Internet surfing. The Internet is an amazing tool for researchers. I don't even remember the last time when I went to the library to find a journal article; not having to walk to the library and search through numerous journals is definitely a huge time saver. And if I have a question about something, it's just a few keystrokes away! However, when you are writing a boring or difficult paper on the computer, it can be extremely tempting to jump onto some of your favorite sites to read the latest news. My favorite news and sports websites are constantly updating new and exciting articles that I'd like to read more about. The thought, "I wonder if they have anything new posted on X site," can lead to hours of off-topic reading. Again, many of these articles can affect you emotionally, thus having a lasting impact on your writing ability that goes beyond just the time spent reading them.

Strategies for Diminishing Distractions

So how do we deal with these technological distractions? Of course, all of these have their place, and in a balanced life they should be enjoyed. However, it takes some discipline to relegate these delightful devils to their appropriate place and not let them get the best of your precious time. One strategy I have found helpful is to cut myself a deal. "Okay, Nate," I say to myself, "If you can turn your phone off and not get on the web from now until noon, then you can indulge for 30 minutes." I cut out all these distractions for a few hours and really go hard on research and writing; then, when I start getting weary and feeling in need of some refreshing diversion, I check my email, Facebook, phone, and favorite websites one right after the other.

Knowing that I'm going to have a fun lunch break with all my favorite intruders helps me stay motivated and keep working until my self-appointed break time. Doing things this way also helps keep emotions under control. By having a set block of time, all the emotions are felt at once rather than being strung out over those hours, reducing the risk of interrupting my flow. Plus, this helps clear my head and prepare me mentally for another few hours of focused research followed by another technology break. Instead of time increments, you may consider having a certain task list and you have to get to a certain point on your list before your next break. At a minimum I would recommend turning off email alerts, especially the little chime that draws you to your inbox. You may also consider using a browser add-on such as "LeechBlock" (for Mozilla) or "Stay-Focused" (for Chrome) that will block websites during your writing times.

Every person is different, so I won't say how long each break should be. If you are a tech addict (as many researchers are), it's probably better to start with shorter periods of focused concentration, and little by little you can begin to lengthen this time so you can build stamina. Eventually you will be able to get some great flow going! Also, you may want to let some of your favorite texting buddies know of your new strategy so they don't get offended when you don't immediately reply. Don't get sucked into believing you can carry on an online conversation with your friend while writing the paper. As mentioned previously, research has found multitasking to be a myth as you don't do either task to full capacity.

Colleagues

Let me say upfront that I think interacting with colleagues regularly is very psychologically healthy and important. I work from home much of the time, so when I am on campus, I very much welcome visitors. However, in excess, such interaction can become a distraction. In any given day, you may have a lot of visitors; perhaps some of these visitors come unannounced and don't take subtle hints you may give for them to leave, or perhaps you very much enjoy talking to the person and find it hard to break away from a mutually enjoyable conversation. Of course, networking is a crucial part of research, and interacting with others can be recharging and strengthening. However, like technology, you need to be the one in the driver's seat making sure that the social aspects of your job don't infringe on your productivity, especially your golden hours.

If you find it hard to get much work done while you're in the office (as I do), you may try working from home. I do nearly all my research and writing from home and find it's where I'm most productive. In graduate school, my advisor had the opposite style and at first he had expectations for me to always be in the office. At one point I had to tell him that if he expected me to come to the office to work all the time, he would have to be happy with much less productivity. When I demonstrated how productive I was from home, he didn't push the issue any more. If you find yourself to be more productive outside of the office, a heart-to-heart with an advisor or department chair will often do the trick, because after all, their best interests are for you to be at your optimal productivity. Some find they are most productive in other settings such as a library or even a coffee shop.

If you are your most productive at the office, you may want to try some strategies for warding off unwelcome visitors. For instance, I have one colleague who lets everyone know when his writing time is each day, since this is a crucial time for him. He demonstrates through this overt action that he intends to keep that time clear from other distractions.

I have another colleague who has a board up next to her office door that notifies would-be intruders what her status is, whether it be "I'm available," "I'm teaching," or "Do not disturb." She effectively lets others know when it is a good time to knock and when it is not. Whatever your method, it's good to find some way to communicate when you are and when you are not available.

Students

It's important to make yourself available to students so you can be a resource and guide for them. However, in some cases, this can be a distraction. If you have to field a lot of student emails, you may want to make a separate email account and let the students know when you'll be checking it. This enables you to answer all the emails at once (even copying and pasting responses if you're getting the same question multiple times), and saves you from having a constant flow of interruptions. Inform your students they need to let you know in advance if they plan on stopping by during your office hours so you don't sit around waiting and being less productive wondering if anyone will come.

Time Your Distractors

It's important to identify which of these distractors is the most harmful for you personally, and then reduce the distractions from that source. O'Hanlon (2007) suggests a great strategy for identifying which ones you struggle with the most: time them. Nothing will motivate you more to change your habits than keeping a careful record of your time and determining how much you are losing to each distractor. Likewise, timing how long you are engaging in a distraction will help you be more aware of it and reduce its impact on your behavior. Can you imagine the impact this had on the professors in Boice's study who thought they were researching for 30 hours and found out that they were indeed only researching 90 minutes? That would certainly motivate me to change!

Chapter Summary

Scholars are not as adroit at managing their time as they often think they are and distractions are a prime reason for this. Distractions can prevent and interrupt flow and diminish your ability to complete a task effectively. Technology distractions can be relegated to breaks and function as a reward for focused effort. Distractions from colleagues and students can be minimized with communication and planning. The final productivity pitfall, described in the next chapter, may be the most destructive of them all.

Chapter 11 Wrap-Up Exercises

1. Write about one or two things you found most helpful in this chapter that you want to apply to your career.
2. Write about a time recently when you experienced flow. Describe the circumstances and what contributed to this state. Also, write about what you can do to increase the frequency of flow in your life.
3. Write about two technology related distractions you struggle with most and what you plan to do to take control of these distractions.
4. What is a people-related distraction you encounter (with colleagues and/or students) and what you can do to minimize this distraction?
5. Complete a time diary (see Appendix B) for a week to see how much time the common distractions mentioned are taking out of your schedule.

12 Deal With Rejection

Main Chapter Points

- How you handle rejection is a key indicator for how successful you will be in publishing.
- If you excessively fear failure, you will be less inclined to submit for publication. You will also be more inclined to submit to lower tier journals, take longer to resubmit manuscripts after being rejected, or simply not submit altogether.
- Fear of failure will prevent you from reaching out and making important professional connections with others that could make the difference in your career.
- Remind yourself you're no worse off for trying.
- Emotionally separate yourself from your work.
- Think 'Next!' when you get rejected, realizing every decent manuscript has a home.
- Keep in mind that publishing is a numbers game and that the most successful scholars get rejected.
- Recognize rejection letters as invaluable feedback that can not only help improve your current manuscript for future resubmission, but can help you develop as a scholar as well.

Chapter Introduction

> Resiliency flowed through Mark's veins and perhaps some of it was genetic. His father was a salesman and was well accustomed to being rejected. In fact, his father had often told him that out of everyone he talked to on a given work day, only 10 of those would listen to his pitch. Of those 10, only one would actually buy what he was selling. During his undergraduate years, Mark spent summers selling pest control and experienced massive amounts of rejection every day. He let that rejection roll off his back and kept pushing forward. Based on what his father had told him, he

> realized selling was simply a numbers game. He also noticed that the top sellers were also the ones out pounding the streets and encountering rejection more frequently. Oftentimes many members of Mark's team couldn't stomach the rejection, quit, and went home early, while Mark made a handsome profit because of his perseverance and ability to accept rejection.
> Mark applied the same lessons from his sales experience to academics. When his manuscripts were rejected, instead of wallowing in grief and self-pity for several weeks, he carefully examined the feedback, noting what was valuable to remember in his revisions and in future studies. Then he'd send it right back to another journal. He noted that many of his colleagues would never try the top journal, which he thought was silly. In the worst case scenario the editor would reject the manuscript and provide some invaluable feedback. He saw that as a plus and wasn't afraid to give it a shot.
> One of his secrets was to not get too emotionally tied up in any certain manuscript, which wasn't too challenging because he was circulating many manuscripts simultaneously. He also pursued several other hobbies and interests so his work wasn't the only thing from which he derived a sense of self-worth.
> Perhaps the most challenging time came when Mark entered the job market in a year when few jobs were available. Based on his success in publishing in graduate school, Mark felt he would quickly succeed in getting a job offer. However, all he received were rejection letters. Rather than let this rejection debilitate him, he decided to work harder than ever and had a marvelous experience as a post-doc. The timing wasn't as he expected, but he did end up getting his dream job.

Billionaire life coach and motivational speaker Tony Robbins (1986) once described what he thinks is the key to success in life. You may be surprised by his answer! He described that the ultimate key to success, wealth, and happiness is achieving massive amounts of rejection. Interesting, why would that be the case? He went on to explain that getting rejected more often means that you are putting yourself out there more often, which is crucial for success. To have success, you have to first try.

A core problem is rejection can be so debilitating for people they will not try again. If you never try, you'll never know if you could have succeeded. That is partly why I believe fear of rejection and how you deal with rejection is one of the most reliable predictors of your ultimate success as a scholar.

Reasons Why Fear of Rejection Impedes Productivity

There are at least four reasons why fear of rejection will harm your productivity as a scholar. These include hindering initial submission, submitting to lower tier journals, not submitting a rejected manuscript for fear it will be rejected again, and not making important social connections.

1 Hindrance of Initial Manuscript Submission

It takes a lot of guts just to submit a manuscript, knowing there's a high probability you will be rejected. I've known so many people that take an unnecessary amount of time on a manuscript and simply don't seem motivated to submit it. I think fear of rejection underlies much of why people do not submit. Most people probably wouldn't admit this, maybe not even to themselves, yet this fear cripples them before they even begin writing.

2 Promotes Submission to Inferior Journals

Many scholars never reach their full potential simply because their fear of rejection causes them to submit manuscripts to lower ranking journals where they believe they have a better chance of avoiding rejection. I will never forget what my advisor said before I submitted a manuscript to my first top tier outlet. He said, "Oh that won't have a chance of getting accepted there." That would have been enough to scare most students out of trying, since on the outset, my article seemed like it was almost surely going to be rejected. Yet, it wasn't. I got it accepted and since then have participated in several radio and newspaper interviews on that work, precisely because it was accepted in a respected journal.

I recently spoke to a professor who served as an editor at a respected mid-tier journal who had just received a "promotion" to become an editor at the top journal in the field of social psychology and was released from his other editorial position. "Wow, I bet you're going to be extremely busy now?" I inquired, assuming his workload was going to be much heavier. "Actually, my editorial load will be significantly lighter at this journal," he replied. "They only have about half the submissions as the journal I edited for previously." Initially, I found it surprising that the top journal would receive half the quantity of submissions as did the less prestigious journal. However, it makes perfect sense to me now—people fear and dread the rejection of highly ranked journals and instead prefer the reduced risk of submitting to lower journals. How many of these articles that were never submitted could have been accepted at the top journal? We'll never know. Even if you have only a remote chance, it's always better to shoot for the stars and miss than to never try. Plus, you'll get great feedback even if you end up submitting to a lower tiered journal later.

3 Fear of Rejection Hampers Resubmission of Rejected Manuscripts

There's no question—rejection is no fun. In fact, research finds that reviewers make "only broad statements—if any—about the positive features of papers" but make an average of nine criticisms per paper (Fiske & Fogg, 1990, pp. 591–592). In Chapter 9, I discussed how there is already a significant lag in the time it takes to get something published, which is out of your control, and how sitting on a rejected manuscript, something you can control, can significantly worsen this lag time and drastically limit your overall productivity. Many scholars take the sting of the rejection so personally that it's difficult for them to even read the review after finding out it was rejected, let alone read it thoroughly enough to make the necessary changes and risk a second (or third, fourth, or even fifth in some cases) rejection.

A very common outcome for the fear of rejection is procrastination. This may even be subconscious, but rejection hurts, so many people will try to delay the pain of facing and acknowledging the rejection that is required for resubmission. This can be especially difficult when a reviewer forgets their decency and makes unnecessarily harsh or personal remarks about your work, which can already be a touchy subject. Believe me, I've experienced this on several occasions. The key is to take into account the reviewer biases that may be influencing the harshness of the comments. Take it with a grain of salt, applying what may be worthwhile as you let the rest of it slide off your back. Don't let that harsh reviewer get the best of you; instead, get that manuscript back out the door—the clock is ticking after all.

4 Impedes Formation of Important Connections

Opportunities to make professional contacts abound, yet many of us never take the leap of faith necessary to reach out because we fear interpersonal rejection. I don't think anyone is immune to this fear, but the most successful scholars are the ones who can overcome it. I'll never forget the anxiety I experienced when I attended my first professional meeting; I was nearly paralyzed with fear and intimidation of meeting people I felt were superior to me. It can help when you realize that other people are nervous too.

One key insight I gained from my postdoctoral advisor (a very prominent researcher in his field) is that even the most senior scholars, who sometimes come across as aloof and uninterested in being contacted by you, are often simply concerned and fearful about their own inability to remember names. In several cases, the seasoned scholars may be as afraid of you as you are of them.

Overcoming the Fear of Rejection and Dealing With It

Hopefully, I've been able to convince you that the fear of rejection is an important issue to handle well. I'd like to start off my discussion of tips for dealing with rejection with a quote by Earl Graves: "We keep going back, stronger, not weaker, because we will not allow rejection to beat us down. It will only strengthen our resolve. To be successful there is no other way." The truly successful scholars find a strengthened, not weakened resolve when they receive rejection. Anyone can deal well with good fortune, but the true test of an individual is how he or she gets up after being knocked down. You can either become better or bitter. Here are a few suggestions that may help upon receiving the inevitable rejections that will come:

1 Remind Yourself That You Have Nothing to Lose

To aid in overcoming the fear of rejection one helpful strategy is to remind yourself that you have nothing to lose (Canfield, 2005). For instance, let's say you decided to apply to Harvard and got rejected. You weren't in Harvard before you applied and you aren't in Harvard after you applied so your life didn't get worse, it stayed the same. You haven't actually lost anything (except a nominal application fee). You've spent your whole life not going to Harvard so you know exactly how to handle that.

2 Separate Yourself Emotionally From Your Work

My undergraduate advisor gave me the valuable suggestion to separate myself from my work. It's often easy to get your ego tied up into what you are writing, but the problem with doing so is that inevitably you will get hurt when your work is criticized (which it surely will be) and rejected (which it very likely will be). If you don't emotionally divorce yourself from what you write it is much easier to let critical words get you down. Just keep in mind that this is simply something you wrote, it is not part of you. You can still be passionate about your work, without becoming emotionally attached to it. If you have several projects going simultaneously (see Chapter 4), it makes it easier to not get overly down when one of them doesn't go your way. Also, if you are living a balanced life and pursuing several other goals (see Chapter 10), it will be easier to emotionally divest from your work because it won't be the only contributor to your self-concept.

3 Just Say "Next!" and Remember That Every Decent Manuscript Has a Home

Canfield (2005), author of *The Success Principles,* wrote the following:

> Get used to the idea that there is going to be a lot of rejection along the way to the gold ring. The secret to success is to not give up. When someone says no, you say, "Next!" Keep on asking. When Colonel Harlan Sanders left home with his pressure cooker and his special recipe for cooking southern fried chicken, he received over 300 rejections before he found someone to believe in his dream. Because he was rejected over 300 times, there are now 11,000 KFC restaurants in 80 countries around the world. (p. 148)

When your manuscript is rejected, rather than fuming about it, the best question to ask yourself and coauthors is, "Which journal should we try next?"

With publishing, a lot of the decision is based on audience fit. Sometimes it is difficult to know exactly which journal is the best fit for your work and it takes some trial and error. Barbara Kingsolver, author of *The Poisonwood Bible,* said the following:

> This manuscript of yours that has just come back from another editor is a precious package. Don't consider it rejected. Consider that you've addressed it "to the editor who can appreciate my work" and it has simply come back stamped "not this address." Just keep looking for the right address.

I strongly believe that every decent manuscript will eventually find a home; it's just a matter of time. For instance, one article, even after being rejected five times previously, found a home in one of the top journals in my field. In fact, one study (Hall & Wilcox, 2007) suggests that 62% of published papers have been rejected at least once and I think the number is higher than that in most fields. Another study found that only 5% of journals reject more than 90% of manuscripts and more journals reject 40–60%. So, the chance of getting a manuscript eventually published is better than you may think (Association of Learned and Professional Society Publishers, 2000). So next time your manuscript is rejected, just say "Next!"

4 It's a Numbers Game

Since it only takes one acrimonious reviewer to doom your article publishing is a crapshoot. You must draw an editor and 2–3 reviewers, none of which have negative biases against your topic. Often it just takes repeated submissions to get the right lineup of people who are favorable to your work. It can really be a numbers game. I recommend choosing three journals that you may want to submit to so that you have a long-term plan for your manuscript, but always start with the top and work your way down.

5 The Most Successful People Get Rejected the Most Often

Sometimes there exists a false notion among those who do not publish frequently that those who are publishing a lot are extremely gifted writers who coast through the review process. In most cases this is completely wrong; I think the most successful scholars are the ones who are submitting work frequently and therefore are probably getting rejected more frequently as well. I have now worked under some of the most prolific psychologists in the field and have observed firsthand how often even these "best and brightest" scholars get rejected time and again. Rejection is very common even for the most famous of authors and their works. Below is a list of some well-known books and how many times they were each rejected before finally being published:

# of Rejections	Book/Author
140	*Jonathan Livingston Seagull* by Richard Bach
38	*Gone With the Wind* by Margaret Mitchell
30	*Carrie* by Stephen King
26	*Watership Down* by Richard Adams
12	*Harry Potter* by J. K. Rowling (Rowling is vague on the number of rejections she got, saying, "I'm not sure if it was a dozen, but it was plenty . . . . "

(Retrieved from http://www.shelflifemagazine.com/archives/004/rejection.html)

English novelist John Creasey received 763 rejection letters before publishing 564 books. I think you get the picture. These authors are now famous because they pushed through the rejection and kept trying. So much of success is simply being persistent. For instance, it is reported that "Stephen King got discouraged and threw out his first few pages of a novel he was working on. His wife rescued it from the trash, wiped off the cigarette ashes, and urged him to stick with it" (O'Hanlon, 2007, p. 41).

6   View Rejection Letters as Free, Priceless Feedback

It may be a nerve-racking thought, but rejection is something that can ultimately make you a better scholar. If you think about it, academia is a great environment to learn how to write and publish well. Every time you submit a manuscript, you have the opportunity to receive free feedback from leaders in the field. In many fields, you would have to pay top dollar to receive this kind of feedback on your work; whereas in academia, you simply need to have the courage to submit something and you can get this feedback for free. The typical journal in my field requires at least 2–3 reviewers and an editor. Given that I currently have 25 manuscripts submitted for publication, I currently have a team of around 75 experts whose job is to provide insight and feedback on what I have written. Let's say the average time academics spend reviewing a manuscript is 4 hours. Can you imagine how much this would cost in the business world or Hollywood to pay 75 experts to take 4 hours of their time to provide a personal consultation? I probably won't make that much money during my entire lifetime. Yet, if I continue at my current pace, I'll constantly have 75 experts helping to improve my work at any given time. What a tremendous resource—and not a penny has been extracted from my bank account (though I suppose I am returning the favor now by serving as an editor and not receiving a penny for that either).

Although I do not always like what reviewers have to say, their feedback is an invaluable resource that has taught me more than I have learned in any of my graduate classes. Canfield (2005) recommends viewing "negative feedback as information about 'improvement opportunities'" (p. 153) and suggests there are three ways of responding to feedback that don't work: caving in and quitting, getting mad at the source of the feedback, or ignoring the feedback. These ineffective strategies for dealing with negative feedback may help you feel better (or forget your bad feelings) for the moment, but none of them will help you in the long term. Remember that you have an invaluable learning resource at your fingertips in the review process. Every author has to deal with an occasional spiteful reviewer whose feedback is not constructive; however, on the whole the feedback is helpful and will improve your research/writing abilities if you try your best to learn from it. Keep in mind that the ultimate goal is having a strong, finished product that has an impact on your field. If you can focus on the quality of the finished product, it will help you to view the rejection letters as aides toward your ultimate goal. Novelist Katherine Patterson once wrote, "I love revision. Where else can spilled milk be turned into ice cream?" The feedback from reviewers can help you to truly transform your research and writing into something fantastic. And it's free!

Chapter Summary

How you handle rejection is a key indicator for how successful you will be in publishing for several reasons. If you excessively fear failure you will be less inclined to submit for publication (and more inclined to procrastinate). You will also be more likely to submit to lower tier journals rather than top tier journals, and lengthen the time it takes to resubmit manuscripts after being rejected. In fact, a fear of failure may prevent you from resubmitting altogether. Fear of failure will prevent you from reaching out and making important professional connections with others that could make the difference in your career. Remind yourself that you're no worse off for trying. Emotionally separate yourself from your work, think "Next!" when you get rejected, and realize that every decent manuscript has a home. Keep in mind that it's a numbers game and that the most successful scholars get rejected. Following these tips will help you to deal with the rejection.

Finally, don't forget to recognize that rejection letters can be an invaluable source of feedback that can not only help improve your current manuscript for future resubmission, but can help you develop as a scholar as well. Nobody likes rejection. The true test of a great scholar is not whether they are rejected or even how often rejection comes, but what they do in reaction to the rejection.

This concludes the broad discussion of how by focusing on priorities, efficiency, and prevention of pitfalls (PEP) you can build a safe, warm home for your academic prosperity. However, depending on where you are at in your career there may be different strategies for applying PEP principles. The following chapters provide very specific suggestions for achieving academic prosperity for people at different stages in their careers.

Chapter 12 Wrap-Up Exercises

1. Write about one or two things you found most helpful in this chapter that you want to apply to your career.
2. Based on what you have read in this chapter, what are the areas in which fear of rejection is limiting you the most?
3. What can you do to minimize the harmful effects of rejection in your life?
4. Rejection can actually be beneficial if you handle it the right way. Write about ways you have benefited from past rejection.

Part IV
PEP at Different Career Stages

Congratulations, you've now learned the basics for how you can achieve ACADEMIC PROSPERITY—academic prosperity through priorities, efficiency, and prevention of pitfalls. The remaining chapters describe how to apply these principles at different phases of your career. Chapters 13–15 focus on students and how to apply PEP principles to get into graduate school (Chapter 13), to shift from the student mentality into a professional mentality (Chapter 14), and to be a good mentee and even become a mentor while in graduate school (Chapter 15). Professors who mentor students would also benefit from these chapters to gain strategies for helping their students to become more productive.

As you find your first academic job, Chapter 16 will help you to get started on achieving academic prosperity. You will learn how to apply PEP principles as a mentor (Chapter 17), as a teacher (Chapter 18), and as a reviewer (Chapter 19). These chapters would also benefit students as they plan for their future careers as professors. The different stages of one's career present different challenges to realizing academic prosperity.

13 Set Up a Productive Graduate Career (Especially for Undergraduates and for Professors Advising Undergraduates)

Main Chapter Points

- Prepare for graduate school by first discovering what interests and excites you.
- Get involved in a research project with a professor on this or a related topic.
- Make sure to prepare well for the GRE, keep your grades strong, and take the types of classes (e.g., research methods and statistics) that will best prepare you for the rigors of graduate school.
- Remember you should select a mentor first, not a university or a graduate program—it's all about who you select.
- Find someone with a productive track record who shares your general research interests and make sure he or she is accepting students.

Chapter Introduction

> Lindsay is in a truly enviable position. She played all her cards just right and received acceptance from seven of the universities to which she applied and four of those programs offered her a high-paying fellowship. Lindsay worked hard as an undergraduate and got very high grades, and she spent months preparing herself for the GRE and received a very high score. Most important, however, Lindsay became very involved in research projects with two professors. Not only did this make her much more appealing to graduate admissions committees, but it helped her to discover what she was most passionate about researching. This self-insight was crucial for her to pick the right graduate program. She did extensive online research to narrow down a number of scholars that did research in the area she was interested in and then checked to see if they were taking students. Lindsay set herself up well to have a very productive career.

This chapter was written for undergraduates who want to begin building a research career. However, graduate students and faculty members will find it contains useful suggestions they may want to share with the undergraduates they are advising or undergraduates in their classes who have expressed interest in graduate school to help them get the best possible start to their research careers.

The foundations for becoming a productive scholar are formed during your undergraduate years. The fact that you are reading this book is a great indicator you are the type of person who wants to start early in planning for success. Undergraduates often take classes without much direction or without much thought of their future, but by getting an early start, you will be a step ahead of the game. This chapter contains suggestions for preparing yourself for graduate school and for selecting a program to ensure you become a successful, productive scholar.

Preparing Yourself for Graduate School

Two of the most important factors that affect your future career are where you go to graduate school and who you work with while there. It's therefore crucial that you make yourself as attractive a candidate as you possibly can to open up as many doors and give yourself as many options as possible. There are several things you can do now to prepare yourself and to make yourself more appealing to future graduate admissions committees.

Find Out What Interests You

Finding out what really gets you excited is very important. You'll want to base your decision of graduate programs largely on who you want to work with and what you want to study, so it's vital to figure out as much as you can now. Think back to some of the classes you've taken up to this point. What classes were most exciting to you and why? Take a wide variety of classes in your area and constantly ask yourself, "Could I spend 5–10 years studying this topic?" You aren't required to have everything completely nailed down, but the better you know what general topics you have an interest in studying, the better you'll be able to make the best decision regarding graduate school.

It's All About Research Experience

Once you have some idea of the general topics that interest you, you'll be able to get some experience doing research under your belt. Or you can go the other direction as well—gaining research experience can help you define what you are interested in. Graduate school is not about classes, it's actually a trade school. You are an apprentice learning the craft of research and publishing. Thus, the BEST way to make yourself an attractive candidate is to have had some practice actually working on and doing the trade. Most undergraduates do not get these kinds of opportunities to begin to develop themselves early, and doing this will put you ahead of the pack. Your research experience (especially if you excel at it and have something to show for it) will make graduate admissions committees put your application in a different stack from everyone else.

I was involved in research as an undergraduate. I had a terrific advisor who helped me to win a small research grant, secure the "Best Student Poster award" at a university competition, and to submit an article for publication. This helped set my application apart. In fact, not only did I get accepted at all seven graduate programs to which I applied, but I received scholarships and financial assistance stipends worth from $150,000 to $250,000 (over 5 years) from each program. I hope you are convinced that research experience can open doors of opportunity for you.

Aside from the great research experience, you will get much stronger letters of recommendation from someone with whom you have done research. I usually agree to write letters of recommendation for my classroom students, but I typically do not know them very well and only have about one indicator of their potential—their grade. However, I have a great deal to write about my research assistant students as I know them much better and have worked much more closely with them. Also, they have typically done a lot to help me personally and thus I feel much more obligated to do a good job for them.

Finding a research opportunity. Oftentimes professors will advertise in their classes or on some kind of bulletin board when they need undergraduates to participate in research opportunities, but don't wait around for opportunities to come your way. Identify a few of the professors you've had whose topics interest you the most and approach those professors. Make sure to do your homework by looking at their curriculum vitae (which is like a resume that includes a list of their publications and can usually be found online by Googling the name of the professor or on the department website) and examining their research interests and publications. If it matches what you are interested in, be proactive and make contact with the first one on your list (preferably in person, perhaps during an office hour). Thank the professor for the class and let them know you are very interested in their topic of research (be specific about what you are interested in). Tell them you are very interested in applying to graduate school in X amount of time and you had really hoped to get some experience doing research. Ask if there is any chance you could help out with any of the projects she is working on. If the answer is no, then ask if there is anyone else in the department or college the professor would recommend contacting. Be persistent and don't give up until you find some kind of opportunity.

Department secretaries, fellow students, and graduate students may also be helpful resources for you. You may not be able to be involved in a project that is directly related to your interest, but any experience is far better than none and you may actually find a topic you hadn't seriously considered initially really interests you once you've been exposed to it.

Set yourself apart as a researcher. Many professors only trust undergraduates to do things that don't require much skill such as data entry, data collection, library runs, etc. These are important parts of the research process; be grateful that you have such an opportunity and excel in any way you can. However, once you have gained respect from the professor or graduate student, ask if there is any way you could be involved more deeply in some aspect of the writing. For example, check if you can help out with the literature review. Making a level of contribution that could merit being an author on a published manuscript will strengthen your application in an amazing way.

Both of the universities I attended had programs set up to help undergraduates to become involved in the research process. For instance, I was able to apply for an undergraduate grant and received $500 to conduct my research. Both universities also had an undergraduate research poster competition. Letting the professor/graduate student you are working with know you are interested in these kinds of opportunities may not only give you the fantastic learning opportunities that come in preparing for such competitions, but also the chance to become involved in the research process more deeply. And who knows, you may even win! However, just participating and being able to list that you participated in such opportunities will set your application apart.

Make Sure to Study Hard for the GRE (Or Major Test in Your Field)

GRE scores (or their equivalent) are quite predictive of success in graduate school and these scores are taken VERY seriously by admissions committees. In fact many programs have cut-off scores, which are good to know in advance to save you money on application fees. Make sure to take the time to prepare yourself. Buy or check out some of the books offered or even take a course. It will be worth the time and effort you put into preparing yourself. Most important, you need to do several practice tests. What ruins the scores of most students is not the questions, but a lack of time to finish. Become acquainted with strategies for answering the questions quickly and effectively, and then practice, practice, practice.

Keep Your Grades Strong

GPA is also strongly considered during graduate school applications, as it not only is a reflection on your intelligence, but also your work ethic and ability to follow through. My advice to you when you get to a Ph.D. program is to stop worrying so much about grades; however, at this stage as an undergraduate, grades remain very important. If you do not have stellar grades, but feel like you have a pretty good excuse (perhaps an illness or personal tragedy), explain this in your cover letter. It may be worth retaking some classes to enhance your GPA.

Don't Wimp Out on the Difficult Classes

One of my regrets as an undergraduate was I tended to take easy classes from professors who wouldn't stretch me as much so I could get a good grade. When I got to graduate school I wished I had taken more of the difficult classes, especially statistics. If you know you might struggle to get a good grade in a certain class (e.g., statistics), consider taking it during your last semester after your transcripts have already been sent out to graduate programs. Very few, if any, will ask you about your grades of your final semester. You may even consider checking to see if there are any graduate classes you might be able to take that would help you to better prepare for graduate school.

Once you have made yourself as appealing as possible to as many programs as possible, it's time to select where you will apply. Make sure to choose the program almost entirely based on one factor: mentor.

Selecting a Graduate Program: It's All About Mentor, Mentor, Mentor

I wish I would have read this book before applying for graduate school. Unfortunately, I let money and the prestige of a program factor into my decision more heavily than mentor. Although the prestige of a program can have some sway (mainly with Ivy League schools), who you worked with and how productive you were with this person will almost always be the most important factor universities consider when you apply for a job at the end of graduate school. Here are some things to consider.

Find Someone With a Current Track Record of Productivity

Probably the most important thing to consider as you explore who to work with is the person's current level of productivity. This is vital because how can someone teach you to do something they haven't yet figured out how to do themselves? The teacher must always be several steps ahead of the learner lest the blind lead the blind into a pit of unproductive joblessness.

To illustrate the importance of choosing someone with a track record of achievement, let me tell you about a friend of mine. In graduate school he paired up with an advisor that had a very slim record of publishing. It's no big surprise that he got hardly anything published at all while he was in graduate school and couldn't find a job. Thankfully, he was able to get a post-doctoral position with a mentor who did have a tremendous record of publishing. It was a night and day difference—suddenly this friend started publishing through the roof. I didn't realize he had it in him and I really believe that so much of the raw talent he had was not being tapped due to the mentor he was stuck with during his five years in graduate school. Fortunately, my friend was able to recover; however, I think most people do not get a second chance like this and never become full-fledged researchers or tenure-track professors. If you become an adjunct professor, you will likely become so buried in heavy teaching loads that you aren't able to establish any kind of publication record.

It's important to find someone who is currently being productive rather than just someone who was productive in the past. Also, check if this person's students are publishing with her. This is important because many scholars (even previously productive ones) fizzle out at the end of their career. You want to avoid at all costs scholars who aren't currently publishing because they will be of little help in training you to be a productive scholar. You'll want to review their curriculum vitae online and examine the last five years of their productivity to get a sense for how they're doing. You may want to ask a trusted professor (preferably your research advisor if you have one) to help you decipher how productive the professor is compared to the norm in your field and also whether the types of journals the professor is publishing in are high quality. You probably won't be able to know this yourself and will want to check with a professor you know about the reputation of the journals. You could also enter the potential professor's name on Google scholar and see if you can find some of his most cited work.

Karen Kelsky, author of the blog *Professor Is In*, suggests finding out how many Ph.D.'s your potential mentor has placed in tenure-track positions over the past several years, which I think is terrific advice. You could do this by directly asking the professor, Googling some of their coauthors and looking for new professors, or by emailing other students in that department.

Contact the Professor

A big mistake that can be made in choosing a graduate program is not contacting the professor(s) you are interested in working with to determine if they have a spot on their team and are interested in you. A friend of mine had four different professors she thought would be a good match for her and thus she thought it was a pretty safe bet that she would end up with one of them. However, she was put with someone she hadn't even heard of and had little interest working with. A lot of heartache could have been avoided for her if she had emailed these professors to see if they would be taking any students, because as it turned out, none of them took a student that year. Also, contacting professors directly could flatter them and make them your advocate in getting accepted into the program. With some programs, if a professor doesn't specifically want to work with you, you won't even get accepted. Many professors don't even consider students who haven't contacted them. If the professor has funding and becomes interested in working with you, this will greatly help your chances of acceptance.

A great place to contact professors could be at a regional or national conference. Make sure you have read their work before you talk to them. Flattery always helps! Now, once you've found a professor who may be interested in taking you on as a student, how do you find out whether this person is someone you would definitely want to work with?

Talk to His or Her Students

One of the most important resources at your fingertips is the professor's current students. Again, conferences might be a good opportunity to talk to these students, or during a campus visit, or often professors will list some of their students on their website. You also could look to see if any of the professors' coauthors show up on the list of graduate students most programs display on their website and email them. Some will be reluctant to tell you how they actually feel about working with their professor because they are worried that their opinion might get back to the professor. Assuring these students their comments are safe with you should help them to open up.

Ask them very pointed questions to get at how the professor is to work with. Some questions you may consider asking are: "How long does it take your professor to give you feedback on your work?" This is imperative to know because some professors get so caught up in what they're doing that they don't make time to mentor and consequently leave their students languishing for months without the students being able to move their work forward.

"What is your professor's work style like? Is she very hands on or hands off?" Depending on the stage you are at, you may want more or less guidance. My first mentor as an undergraduate was very hands on, teaching me each step of the research process and guiding me through; this was very helpful at that stage when I didn't know what I was doing. My graduate professor was very hands off, which was okay because I had a better handle on things by then and actually enjoyed the autonomy he gave me. You may have some idea of what your style is like and what might be the best match for you. Also, although a mentor may be hands off, ask about the lab. It could be that other students in the lab might be very helpful at walking you through the necessary learning steps in the research process.

"What do you like best about working with your professor? What do you like least about working with them?" Starting off with the positive is a good way to go and can help identify some helpful strengths. Speaking positively first may help a student feel more comfortable confiding about some of the difficulties of working with this professor.

"Does your professor let you take the lead on some manuscripts?" This is also a very good question to ask because I had a friend whose advisor was trying to get tenure and made him do the majority of the work on a paper and then would always be the first author. Depending on your field, you're going to need to be first author on some articles and thus it's important to work with someone who will let you lead out and not make you his peon. You may check with your current mentor to make sure about the norms of your particular field however.

"Does your professor help you connect with other scholars in the field?" This is helpful because so much of what you gain from your advisor are the connections they have, and if they aren't willing to share this network with you, you will lose out. The connections your advisor has could be instrumental in getting you a job. These are a few of the questions you should ask the students of the professors with whom you are hoping to work.

A Few Other Things to Consider

Hopefully you have multiple offers of where you can attend graduate school with mentors that are a good match. If they offer you the chance to come for a visit, definitely make arrangements to do so. Even if they don't officially offer this, it doesn't hurt to ask. There's only so much you can do by phone and email; getting an in-person visit is crucial to making the best decision. Remember, not only do the next five to six years hang in the balance, but your entire career—even the rest of your life, will be affected in a profound way by this decision. Therefore, the more information you can collect to help you make a good decision, the better.

Again, all the other things I mention in this section should take a back seat to a good match with a mentor. However, if you have multiple offers, there could be other factors you'll consider. One is whether the professor you want to work with has their own funding (or grant money to conduct research). If they do, this is a big advantage because it could open up additional time for you to do research and be funded from their grant. You'll want to know how much teaching/research you'll be responsible for and would probably want to go to the place where you'd have the lightest teaching load. When it comes down to it, hiring committees care much more about your publication record than they do about your teaching record (unless you don't apply to research extensive universities).

You'll want to find out how rigorous the program is and how much coursework is required. Some programs shoot themselves in the foot by making the classes so hard and so rigorous that their students can't spend sufficient time researching and learning how to do the real trade they've been hired to do as graduate students. Similarly, you'll want to find out what the opportunities are to learn statistics or whatever tools are relevant for your field. Some programs may not offer the types of classes that would help you gain the tools to help you excel in a field that has increasingly rigorous publication requirements.

Finally, the amount of scholarship money, travel money, living stipend, as well as the geographic location should play into your decision, but the mentor should be the biggest factor. Remember if you get paid a bit less (or don't get paid at all depending on your field) or are in a place geographically you aren't as fond of, it's all worth the investment if you have the right mentor. Getting a little more at one school may not be worth getting a much higher starting salary later on. Remember graduate school is an investment in your future and thus you might as well invest in that which promises to pay the highest return on your investment. A couple thousand dollars extra in student loans or putting up with cold weather is worth it to give your career the best chance to take off. And, you may find you end up really liking that part of the country.

Spread Your Wings and Go to a Different Place

A final note is that oftentimes we get comfortable with the institution where we received our undergrad degree. Perhaps it's close to parents or we've made a lot of friends there and we may just think we want to go there. I would strongly discourage you from getting your Ph.D. from the same institution where you got your undergraduate degree for a few reasons.

For one, an important resource you bring with you to a future job will be the contacts you make. If you stay at your undergraduate institution, you won't be able to make as many contacts to offer to a potential employer. This is especially important if you want to one day return to teach at your undergraduate institution. Most top research universities do not hire from among their own graduate students.

Another bonus of going elsewhere is your perspective is broadened as you get to see how other programs are run and compare it to what you have been learning at your previous institution. Comparing these systems will help you to know how you might want to run things when you are a professor or a department chair. You gain the chance to develop an entire network of friends and colleagues you never would have experienced or learned from otherwise. If the timing is such that you are very reluctant to leave, you may consider getting your master's degree at your home institution, but don't stay for your Ph.D. You'll be glad you left, trust me.

Once you have been accepted to your best fitting program, you are on your way to publishing success. Make sure to read the tips especially for graduate students and review the rest of the principles in this book frequently. Good luck on this exciting adventure of your life!

Chapter Summary

If you are reading this book as an undergraduate, you are light years ahead of your peers and there is a great deal you can do right now to prepare yourself for becoming a productive scholar. Your first step is to prepare yourself in every way you can for graduate school. You can do this by discovering what interests and excites you, then get involved in a research project with a professor. Make sure to prepare well for the GRE, keep your grades strong, and take the types of classes (e.g., research methods and statistics) that will best prepare you for the rigors of graduate school.

Remember you are selecting a mentor first, not a university or a graduate program—it's all about who you select. Find someone with a productive track record who shares your general research interests, make sure she is accepting students, talk to at least one of those students to find out what it's like working for this professor, consider several other more minor factors, and don't be afraid to spread your wings and go somewhere far away from home. Once you get accepted to graduate school, the next chapter will provide you with essential information about how to approach this very different career phase.

Chapter 13 Wrap-Up Exercises

(Depending on where you are in the process, these exercises may not be completed in one sitting, but can help guide you through the process.)

1. Write about one or two things you found most helpful in this chapter that you want to apply to your career.
2. Write about some topics you are particularly interested in studying.
3. Examine the vitae of some of the professors in your department. Find 2–3 of them that match your interest. What are their names and topics? What is your plan to approach them regarding research opportunities (e.g., email, drop by during office hours, etc.)?
4. What is your plan to prepare yourself for the GRE or other graduate entrance exam?
5. What are some classes in your major that would prepare you well for the rigors of graduate school?
6. Based on your research of graduate schools and professors, who are three professors with whom you could see yourself working?
7. Describe the conversation you had with each professor and rate how interested, on a scale from 1–10, this person might be in working with you. Also note how they responded (yes or no) to your question about whether they are taking on any students next year.
8. What comments did the students of each of these professors make in regards to what it's like working with professor X, Y, and Z?
9. What are some of the other important considerations you are taking into consideration regarding your top three programs?

14 From Graduate Student Mentality to Professional Mentality

Main Chapter Points

- Graduate school is an apprenticeship and should focus primarily on research, not on coursework or even on your thesis alone.
- Change your paradigm by switching from a "student" mentality to a "professional" mentality.
- View your graduate experience as a job and come to "work" each day by working on the research.
- Beware that course grades, long undergraduate breaks, limited pay, and even university milestones like theses and dissertations will tempt you to revert to your undergraduate mindset.

Chapter Introduction

> Jill had straight A's all through her years as undergraduate and was able to get scholarships at every graduate program to which she applied. She had always stressed about her grades and it was paying off for her now as she accepted an offer at one of the top programs in her field. Getting such great grades as an undergrad gave her a feeling of accomplishment that she was determined to graduate with a Ph.D. and a 4.0 GPA. Not only did she want to get good grades, but she wanted to graduate at the top of her class. She sought to do better than everyone else, but this was difficult because her program had cream of the crop students who also excelled as undergraduates. In order to keep up and stay ahead she had to double her efforts and really work hard. At the end of the semester she was so relieved to be done with class after working so hard, that she just needed a break. Jill's drive, however, motivated her to not relax, but instead she bought her books for next semester's classes and read through them so she'd be prepared.
>
> She noticed her advisor didn't ask her to do a lot, but when he did, she would reply back in a timely manner. She was too busy with class

> to begin any of her own projects, but felt somewhat part of the research process as she looked up references for her advisor and did other little tasks he had asked her to do. Jill felt like things were going well. In fact, she had even spent one evening brainstorming some ideas for her dissertation project. This would be an extremely daunting task and would stretch her and prepare her for the future, when her career would begin.
>
> In due time, Jill accomplished her goals and surpassed her classmates. She achieved her 4.0 GPA and did indeed graduate at the top of her class. Although it was a very difficult project, Jill felt great about her dissertation and was confident that she would now be able to publish it. That's why she was confused when she couldn't seem to find a job. Hadn't she done everything just right?

The term "graduate school" is an incorrect or unsuitable name for this post bachelor experience. The label of "graduate school" incorrectly leads people, like Jill, to believe that the objective of graduate school is to continue one's education through schooling. When most people hear the word "school," they think of a building in which lectures are delivered.

The "school" part of graduate school misleads people into thinking that classes are the central aspect of this graduate experience. As a result, most people who enter and complete graduate school naturally consider themselves to be "students." What is the primary role of a "student" you might ask?—to excel in coursework, which is probably what you did as an undergraduate "student," right? Regrettably, this is about the only accomplishment of graduate students who do not realize that the primary objective of graduate school is to learn to produce research, rather than to simply read and critique research others have done. Similarly, new professors may begin their careers considering themselves to be primarily teachers. Unfortunately, universities in America unintentionally promote this focus by concentrating heavily on coursework and teaching. This results in misleading graduate students and new professors into thinking coursework and teaching are the main points of their experience.

The emphasis on coursework should end when you receive your bachelor's degree and be replaced with an entirely different type of education during your graduate experience—an apprenticeship. The apprenticeship system was first developed in the later Middle Ages and consisted of a novice receiving training in a skilled trade (such as carpentry) at the hands of a master teacher. Most of this training was done on the job. The novice learned by doing the job while being guided and corrected by the master. This is how an apprenticeship should be conducted. However, in the current educational system, apprenticeships can go awry. The objective of the graduate experience is to learn to become a productive, independent researcher. Thus, a more appropriate term for graduate school would be "professional training" or a "professorial apprenticeship."

To illustrate how students can get so caught up in what they think they're supposed to be doing that they neglect their primary purpose, let's discuss the case of Jack. Jack spent five years as an apprentice to a master carpenter. During this time Jack became familiar with several of the renowned books describing different theories and techniques on how best to build a house. In fact, Jack became so proficient in the carpentry literature that he could fluently critique several of the prominent theories in a way that was impressive to an entire committee of carpenters. However, Jack spent so much time reading and critiquing what had been written by others about carpentry that he had very little time left to observe and work closely with the master carpenter. In fact, he hadn't actually built much of anything himself, as reading and critiquing others' work had consumed nearly all of his time. He thought he was doing everything he was supposed to, having been lauded by other carpenters for his great knowledge on the subject. After all, is that not the point of schooling, to learn all you can about your chosen field of study?

Now let's say you are looking for someone to build a house, what are the chances you would hire Jack to build it for you? I'm not suggesting that it isn't important to become familiar with the literature or relevant theories of your field, but at the end of the day, you've got to be able to show you can do something with what you've learned. The best way to learn how to do research is to DO research. You must be able to demonstrate to future employers not only that you know how to independently create something, but that you have done so multiple times and in multiple different ways. Your dissertation having been your first foray into independent research is like Jack having built his first table. It may be a handsome looking table, but you're needed for much more than a table. Furthermore, universities need someone who is capable of immediately training their own team of "professionals" in this very specialization, so how can you trust someone with such a task who has just built his first table (no matter how much he has read up on carpentry)?

Shifting Your Paradigm

Hopefully by this point it's clear that being a graduate professional is much different than being an undergraduate student, yet many never fully make this paradigm shift. What exactly is a paradigm shift? Thomas Kuhn (1962) used the term "paradigm shift" to describe changing one's basic assumptions within the ruling theory. Unfortunately the American graduate system, with its strong focus on coursework, actually reinforces the paradigm that graduate school should be about coursework. Heavy course loads make it particularly difficult for people to focus on what matters most—becoming a professional who is learning by actively doing actual research. When you begin to perceive yourself as a professional rather than as a student, there will be some key changes in how you prioritize your time and your overall approach to research. I offer several suggestions for successfully making this transition by contrasting the student mentality with the professional mentality in several important areas.

Your Career Begins on Your First Day in Graduate School

The way you view your graduate experience will go a long way in determining how you approach it. I will contrast the student mentality with the professional mentality in this dimension.

Student mentality. Those with the "student" mentality treat the graduate school experience as an extended probationary or waiting period until their profession actually begins. 'My career begins when I get my first tenure-track position,' they reason. As a result, they procrastinate and don't seriously begin doing the very work they have been hired to learn to do on-the-job; like Jack the carpenter, they spend all their time reading and critiquing the work others have done. They squander the master's time, because you can't learn to build a house if you aren't willing to commit significant time every week for several years to build it.

Let's face it, crafting a well-designed and well-written research article is a complicated, multi-phase process. Learning how to do this well takes years and years of experience of actually doing it while being guided and corrected by a master. Yet, many do not seriously begin the actual research process until their theses or dissertations and in the competitive world we live in, this is far, far too late. Many confuse job enhancement workshops with their job and fail to show up to do what their employers want them to do, spending all their time preparing for the enhancement workshops.

Professional mentality. Conversely, professionals understand that their careers begin upon entering graduate school and everything they do will count on their permanent record. Thus, the first shift professionals make is realizing their graduate experience is not school, but a job. They know they can't possibly get promoted in the future if they don't show up for their current job—that would be crazy! Professionals recognize what their job is (research), and what their objective is (conducting and writing up research), and they show up to work every day, not just once or twice a week when they don't have classes (enhancement workshops) scheduled. They shift their priorities to ensure that they can do the job, which is their primary purpose for being there.

Common Obstacles in the Transition From Student to Professional

By now you've probably decided that it's in your own best interest to shift your perspective from being a student to becoming a professional. However, there are obstacles that will try to lure you back into student mode. To make a complete transition, you will need to face these foes, some of which are deeply ingrained habits formed during your years as an undergraduate student. They include grade anxiety, long student breaks, and university milestones (e.g., master's thesis, dissertation, etc.). Each of these represents a trap that can tempt you to retreat back into student mode. I'll now discuss each one and make some suggestions on how to resist their allure.

Free Yourself of Grade Anxiety

Grade anxiety is perhaps the most widespread of all the obstacles you will face, precisely because you wouldn't be in graduate school if you hadn't been concerned about your grades. It has been deeply woven into your system for years and you likely even derive part of your sense of self-worth based on your ability to get A's in your classes. I was personally afflicted with a large dose of grade anxiety, especially as an undergraduate. I was the type of student who would set up appointments with professors after nearly every test to argue with them about why my answer should have received credit. The term "grade grubber" would have described me to a tee. I worked very hard in all my classes and could often be found at the library at 11:45 p.m. when loud music was blared through the speakers, signaling the close of the library was imminent. Looking back, I think it was entirely appropriate to have this mentality as an undergraduate student. Doing so helped me get good grades and an acceptance to graduate school.

Then, I made a paradigm shift thanks to a wise advisor who came from the British system in which they did not even hold regular classes. He often suggested that the best scholars find a way to make classes something they do in the background while their main focus is the research. I have found that tasks often take the amount of time you give to them. Thus, if you put class assignments first, they will often chew up all of your time. When I finally freed myself of grade anxiety, it was like a breath of fresh air. It was as if shackles were taken off of my wrists and I was free at last. Of course you need to do well enough to get by, but I have always found there is a HUGE difference in the effort required to get an A versus an A−, or to get a B+ versus an A−. I still wanted to do decently and my program (like most) required at least a B to pass. However, I found it liberating when I got a B+ and it didn't bother me. However, you may want to put a bit more effort into classes in which you have a professor who may write you a letter of recommendation. Also, don't take this suggestion as a pass to shirk. If you aren't doing a great deal of research, lower grades will only hurt you overall.

One thing that helped me dispel my grade anxiety was realizing the scorecard is totally different in graduate school and few in the future will even care to ask you about your grades in graduate school. Unless you are working on a terminal master's degree, you won't be applying to another program and you'll rarely, if ever, be asked for your grades by future employers, whose primary concern is whether you have learned to produce quality research. In fact, grades aren't included on your all-important curriculum vitae. In his book chapter entitled, "A Guide to Ph.D. Graduate School: How They Keep Score in the Big Leagues," Charles Lord (2004) writes the following:

> Since I have been in my department, we have hired more than half the current faculty. I have been intensively involved in all of these searches, both during the time I was department chair and later. Would it surprise you to know that I have never seen the graduate transcript of any of my

colleagues? We do not request a transcript of graduate grades because my colleagues and I would regard that information as useless. We are trying to hire the best scholars, not people who got the best grades in their graduate courses. (p. 10)

My experience on the job market confirms Dr. Lord's words. I applied to many programs while I was on the job market, and only once was I asked for my transcript. You have already demonstrated your academic ability by getting into and completing graduate school and that is probably partly why nobody even asks for your grades. You've shown that you have the smarts and now employers want to see what you can build. Your handiwork is ultimately the best proof of a successful apprenticeship.

As a note of caution, you may need to put more emphasis on grades as a first year graduate student. It's important to gain your bearings and to make good first impressions. Make sure you are doing well that first year as you get your feet wet in the research and then you can gradually make more and more of a shift to a stronger research focus.

Avoid the Allure of the Long, Undergraduate Breaks

People with a student mentality are extremely relieved when finals are over and they check out for the entire holiday recess or even for the entire summer until class begins again. Those with a professional mentality are also relieved when finals are over, but for a different reason—they are excited to have a lot more time to devote to their primary goal—doing research. Finals are simply a distraction from what they are really focused on, which is conducting high caliber research. They never took a complete break from the research during the semester, but were frustrated by not having as much time as they wanted to push their research agenda forward. Now I'm definitely not suggesting being a workaholic—a good balance is crucial to productivity. However, when I looked around at my older siblings and friends who had "real" jobs, I noticed that none of them were taking a four week break in December, rather they had about a week off and then they began working again. Students who get caught up in their classes during the semester and don't have time for research tend to be the most unproductive. If they also check out between semesters, then papers that they collected data for all semester never get written, and their work as a graduate student is wasted.

The Potentially Counterproductive University "Milestones"

The purpose of university milestones such as a master's thesis or dissertation is to try to rehabilitate those students who have been sucked in to the "school" aspect of graduate school, which is most students given the heavy course loads most face. It is designed to help those like carpenter Jack to experience their first foray into applying knowledge by doing something. Despite all the lost time in filling out endless amounts of paperwork, getting signature after signature, and working through the hoops and loops of the bureaucracy, these milestones can be helpful because you get feedback from an entire committee on your work.

Yet, if you take the wrong approach to these milestones they can be a major hindrance to your progress. Once early on in my program. I began setting up and running several studies in a computer lab where many students came to work. I'll never forget the question so many students asked me, "So is this for your master's thesis or your dissertation?" They just assumed I wouldn't be doing research for the sake of publishing and any research done by a student should be devoted toward one of these end goals. I knew this because of the surprise and even confusion written on their faces as I told them I was just doing it for the sake of getting published. So many people stuck in the student mentality are similarly limited by this view that all research done during graduate school should be directed toward achieving one of these milestones.

Conversely, the professionals consider these milestones to be just another project they have to check off their list. My advisor always told me that if I had enough research going on, I could be free to simply pick whichever project was at the right stage and call it my dissertation. Students build up the dissertation as being this monstrous project that they should devote years to completing. When they complete this one project, they feel they have accomplished a great feat which artificially inflates their sense of accomplishment. They have stressed about it and spent so much of their time fussing over it that once it's complete they feel justified in taking a long break from research. Also, because their dissertation is their main objective, if the data don't support their hypotheses, they feel crushed.

By many accounts, my dissertation failed. I was too ambitious and included six experimental conditions in a massive longitudinal intervention study that didn't pan out according to my hypotheses. Was I devastated? Not at all, I had too many other studies going on to worry much about it. In fact, I included other things in my data collection and some of them did work out. I have since submitted manuscripts from this otherwise failed project. My main emotion at the time was frustration, knowing that I had to spend so much time writing up null results that were not publishable. You should learn from my mistake and do a project that is not overly complex: one that has a very good chance of working out so that you don't lose all that time in writing un-publishable findings.

Many advisors may not agree with viewing the dissertation in this way and you do not want to upset your advisor. Make sure to discuss this with your advisor to make sure you are on the same page.

Working for Pay Versus Working for Your Future

Most graduate positions may have a set number of hours they expect you to work for a research assistantship. A student can get caught up in punching a time clock and never going over the "official" hours. A professional ignores any time barriers and puts in far more time than they are paid. Most salaried workers (usually the higher paid people in society) are not punching time clocks; instead, they are striving to do everything that needs to be done to make an excellent product. This is the type of mentality for which you should strive. Do not get caught in the trap of actually limiting yourself to the "official" hours you are required to work. This could lead to dissatisfaction for working more than your allotted time.

Graduate school is the time to be future-minded. As a graduate student, I often put in several hours of unpaid work on research every week simply because I knew that everything I did would count toward my future career and I would eventually receive a payout for what I did.

This type of mindset can yield large dividends. Recall the study of Mischel that began in the 1960s. He offered hungry 4-year-olds a marshmallow as they waited in an empty room. They were told that if they could wait 15 or 20 minutes for the experimenter to return, they could have two marshmallows. Most of the children indulged (about 66%), but there were some that held out for the bigger prize. The children were surveyed 10 years later and those that resisted the tempting marshmallow were described as more competent and had higher test scores than those who had indulged (Shoda, Mischel, & Peake, 1990). Just the fact that you came to graduate school means you are more like the children that held out for the bigger prize, so don't spoil it now by getting caught up with how many hours you are officially paid; work for the distant future. The more time you can spend on research the better. Although you may not see an immediate reward for the hours you put into your research, there will be a payoff eventually in the way of getting your first job, getting tenure more quickly and easily, and getting future promotions down the road.

Chapter Summary

By putting such a heavy emphasis on coursework, most universities in America mislead students into thinking that graduate school is about classes. As a result, many graduate students get their Ph.D. without having done a substantial amount of research and are underprepared for the real world of academia where they must do independent research. You can avoid this fate by changing your paradigm and switching from the "student" mentality to a "professional" mentality. This includes viewing your graduate experience as a job and coming to "work" each day by working on the research. It becomes important to prioritize your schedule so that you put the research first and the job enhancement classes second. Also know that certain things will tempt to you revert to your undergraduate mindset: course grades, long undergraduate breaks, limited pay, and even university milestones like theses and dissertations. Hopefully, you will resist their allure, always consider yourself a professional, and behave accordingly.

In this chapter, I emphasized the crucial role of apprenticeship and the right mindset to adopt as you approach this role. However important the right approach and priorities are, it's imperative for your ultimate success in graduate school to internalize some key strategies for being an excellent mentee as described in the next chapter. You will also learn how to begin mentoring others as you progress.

Chapter 14 Wrap-Up Exercises

1. Write about one or two things you found most helpful in this chapter that you want to apply to your career.
2. Why do you think it is important to make the paradigm shift from graduate student to professional?
3. Write some of your ideas for how you can best make this important paradigm shift.
4. What are the two biggest things that might distract you from fully making this transformation in your approach to graduate school?

15 The Graduate Student Guide to Be a Great Apprentice, Seek Mentorship, and Become a Mentor

Main Chapter Points

- People are your most valuable resource for being a productive scholar.
- Adopt a humble, "How can I improve?" mentality as you strive to be an outstanding apprentice.
- If your advisor doesn't provide critical feedback, solicit it from him or her.
- Seek additional mentorship from advanced graduate students and post-docs, your committee members, and the outside collaborators of these individuals.
- Seek to become a mentor for other students.

Chapter Introduction

> Bill doesn't like to be told what to do. In fact, it's very difficult for him to follow someone else's lead, and therefore mentoring him has been a challenge for his graduate advisor. To make matters worse, Bill is also very sensitive and if someone criticizes one of his ideas, he reacts defensively. For example, when his advisor points out advisor pointed out that he needs to work on organizing his arguments more effectively his arguments. Instead of applying this feedback and improving, Bill complains to his fellow graduate students about what a jerk his advisor is. Because of this, Bill essentially cuts himself off from valuable feedback that could make a big difference in his professional career. Bill resists information that could make him a much better scholar and writer.

Mentorship is important at all phases of the research career, whether you are a graduate student, a new professional, or even a seasoned scholar. As I mentioned, graduate school should be termed a "professorial apprenticeship" because the whole purpose is to learn the craft of research as best you can at the hands of a master teacher. Hopefully you selected an advisor who is productive because it's hard to teach someone else when you yourself have never had, or no longer possess, the motivation to be productive. For instance, if a carpenter got a job teaching without having built much of anything, it would be hard for him to effectively teach others. If your advisor isn't very productive as a scholar, don't despair, you can possibly switch advisors or at least gain informal mentorship from others. In fact, besides describing how to be a great apprentice, the second objective of this chapter is to discuss ways to seek mentorship. Finally, whether you are a student or new professional, it's never too early to begin mentoring others.

Being a Great Apprentice

A key attribute of an apprentice is someone who has a true desire to grow and improve. If you really want to develop well as a scholar, you've got to want to improve and be willing to undergo the chisel and have your rough edges broken off, which can be a bit painful. Here are a few tips for being a terrific apprentice.

Ask for Feedback and Suggestions for Improvement

The whole point of an apprenticeship program is for you to learn on the job, and that means learning from your own mistakes. Many have the mixed blessing of an advisors who are critically minded and not afraid to tell you exactly what they think. Of course this kind of person may be somewhat difficult to work with, but if you handle the feedback with humility and an attitude of wanting to improve, the long-term benefits may be considerable. If, however, your advisor is not the type to offer much criticism or feedback, it's your job to seek it out. It may sound absurd to ask about what you can do to be a better scholar from someone who doesn't appear to have any issues with you, yet doing so will help you to obtain the information you need to make course corrections now. It's much better to learn these things now while the stakes are low than to have to learn it later when your job may be on the line. Furthermore, according to Kram (1983), students who ask for assistance or criticism come across as more assertive and competent to their mentors.

Canfield (2005), author of *Success Principles*, suggests:

> Most people are afraid to ask for corrective feedback because they are afraid of what they are going to hear. There is nothing to be afraid of. The truth is the truth. You are better off knowing the truth than not knowing the truth. Once you know it, you can do something about it. You cannot fix what you don't know is broken. You cannot improve your life, your relationships, your game, or your performance without feedback.
>
> But what's the worst part of this avoidance approach to life? You are the only one who is not in on the secret. The other person has usually already told [others] . . . what they are dissatisfied with . . . Most people would

rather complain than take constructive action to solve their problems. The only problem is they are complaining to the wrong person. They should be telling you, but they are afraid of your reaction. As a result, you are being deprived of the very thing you need to improve your relationship, your product, your service, your teaching, or your parenting. (p. 158)

Canfield then suggests actively soliciting feedback by asking something like, 'On a scale from 1 to 10, how would you rate the quality of my performance during the past semester?' Any answer less than 10 should be followed with a question such as 'What would it take to make it a ten for you?' He points out that it's important to show gratitude, rather than defensiveness, for the feedback so the person doesn't regret having shared his feedback with you. Humbly applying corrective feedback is key for successfully navigating your role as the apprentice.

Be Motivated and Productive

There aren't many things that will make an advisor happier than having his student actively working to produce research with his advisor's name included on it. Advisors get frustrated when the joint research projects they have invested in continually get delayed due to class assignments or other obligations. This situation is equivalent to a boss paying an employee even though she continually misses work: that's frustrating. The principles in this book should help you avoid these issues. If you are done with a project and have nothing to work on, be proactive and ask your advisor if there is anything they would like you to work on, since they are probably busy and may not realize you are free. Seek out projects that might be useful and approach your advisor with such ideas. This type of proactive student is an invaluable resource to a swamped advisor. Plus, the advisor will be impressed.

Be Considerate of Your Advisor's Time

Most academics have a lot of duties to perform, many meetings to sit through, and diverse conferences to attend throughout the country and world. Be considerate of their time and try to avoid throwing bombs in their laps (i.e., things that need immediate attention) by preparing well in advance of deadlines and meetings. This is also why it is helpful to have multiple projects going simultaneously (see Chapter 6) so you're not left twiddling your thumbs as you wait for a response. Also, when you meet with your advisor, remember that his time is valuable. I suggest having a written agenda of things you want to discuss to ensure nothing important is forgotten and that the meeting runs efficiently.

Seeking Mentorship

Many graduate students think narrowly and do not realize that some needed mentoring experiences await them outside of their primary advisor. New professionals may be hesitant to seek a mentor because they think that was all part of graduate school and there's no need for more mentorship. Your advisor may be a superstar, but is limited to one set of experiences and skills. If your advisor is possessive and would perceive any outside seeking as unfaithfulness, a heart-to-heart talk may be necessary. Otherwise, it's a very prudent decision to extend the network of people who can teach you valuable insights. The following are some suggestions of where you might look and how you might approach such a person.

Start With Advanced Fellow Students or Post-docs

The low-hanging fruit and probably the most likely people to give you their time and mentoring are advanced graduate students and/or post-docs. I suggest doing some homework first and identifying a person who has a track record for being productive (otherwise you may be wasting your time) and whose research interests are at least close to yours. Depending on your personality, you could approach this person directly and let them know you admire what they've accomplished and would appreciate their mentorship. I had a junior graduate student approach me like this and I must say I was flattered and immediately became very invested in helping her. Or, you could take a more subtle approach and discuss an idea for mutual collaboration. Whichever approach best fits your style, this is a good place to start.

I attribute a great deal of the success I have experienced to the mentoring I received from both an advanced graduate student and later a post-doc. My graduate student friend helped me design my first experiments, decide what measures to use, learn to prepare surveys, etc. He also connected me with his advisor (who later became my postdoctoral advisor) and with a new professor who has turned out to be one of my core collaborators. Then came a post-doc who shared many of my interests. He helped me to design rigorous control conditions and design my first long-term intervention study. This laid the groundwork for getting my first top tier publications. He patiently walked me through the basics of manuscript preparation and taught me a lot about statistics. He also introduced me to his graduate advisor with whom I later published. Although both of these outstanding individuals invested a lot of time and effort in helping me, I was able to return the favor by involving them in my resulting publications.

That is one of the great things about academia—it can foster a real win-win mentality and provides compelling rewards for those willing to provide guidance. I highly recommend sharing authorship with collaborators if that is acceptable in your field. Of course, you want to follow ethical guidelines, which would exclude someone who did next to nothing; however, if the person made a substantive contribution (and if your particular field doesn't frown on multiple authors), by all means, add them as an author to your paper without hesitation. If you are good at involving others in your papers, they will involve you in theirs.

Committee Members Can Also Be Helpful Mentors

When you select professors to serve on your thesis or dissertation committees, do so carefully and with a broader picture in mind. Choose individuals who have a track record of productivity, for these individuals may not only give valuable feedback on your university milestones, but could become valuable mentors and collaborators. Ask them to add to a paper you are writing or check with them if there is a project they could use some help with; it's a great way to bring them into your network. They could also help connect you with scholars outside your university that share your research interests.

Offer Something of Value to Someone You Admire to Recruit Them as a Mentor

Those you associate with at your university should have collaborative networks of their own you should attempt to tap into. Check out the curriculum vitae of these individuals to see who they are working with and talk to your contacts about an idea you have that could include a particular person. A few examples could include someone that is savvy in statistics (or some other skill), someone with strong writing abilities, or someone with access to resources (such as research participants or some specialized machinery). It's especially helpful if you have something of value (such as those items mentioned above) you may be able to offer this person as well.

For example, the advanced graduate I mentioned earlier introduced me to a very productive new professor at another university. This new professor is constantly in search of good data. I had access to an enormous subject pool. I actually ran several studies that included variables he was interested in and even gave him the opportunity to design a massive study I would run for him. I learned so much from him in the process of collecting the data and helping to write up the studies based on our findings. He has not only become one of my best collaborators, but has also connected me with several other leading scholars in my field. This career altering mentorship experience came about thanks to an introduction from another mentor and because I was willing to do extra work to provide him with something he valued. Having connections to bright and productive scholars is paramount to your success in publishing, and if you wait until you graduate to make connections outside your university, you'll have missed some incredibly valuable mentoring. However, although it's good to attempt to make these kinds of connections, it is highly uncommon to be able to do so successfully without a shared connection with someone else like your advisor, so don't get discouraged if it doesn't work out.

Become a Mentor

My dad loved a certain quote by Confucius and made it his motto: "He who wishes to secure the good of others, has already secured his own." It may seem counterintuitive that taking so much of your time to help someone else could yield such enormous benefits to yourself, but it's a true principle. Mentoring is a win-win situation and I think this is especially true in academia where collaboration is vital.

I was actively involved in learning as much as I could from those around me. Once I began to get a grasp on some of the key principles of doing good research, I had the desire to pay it forward and help mentor others. I didn't want to wait until I became a professor to engage in the thrilling process of helping to nurture the research career of another.

I had already begun using undergraduate research assistants to help me collect data and code video interactions. I decided to choose some of the most promising students and form a "writing team." At my graduate institution, it was unheard of for undergraduates to be involved in anything other than very menial tasks. I didn't believe this was a useful paradigm, probably because my undergraduate mentor involved me in writing manuscripts for publication. So, I asked my writing team of five undergraduates to come up with research questions and began to walk them through the research process.

By some accounts my first attempt to mentor others did not go so well. Although all five students had each committed to staying on the writing team for at least two semesters, all but one of them dropped out after the first semester. I was frustrated and wondered if my time and effort was in vain since the projects that had been initiated were not brought to fruition. Nonetheless, in hindsight, it was worth it because the one who stayed learned some important skills and kept working with me for two full years. In fact, she was motivated and proved to be an outstanding apprentice. It was exhilarating to watch her grow as a researcher and by the end of her time with me, she had received acceptance at a terrific graduate program and won every research award available to undergraduates at our university. Furthermore, we've established a strong collaborative tie that will be a major advantage to both her and my overall productivity.

I was presented the opportunity to expand my mentorship to fellow graduate students as one new student approached me with a request that I mentor her (as I had previously mentioned). I actively recruited two other promising graduate students to our lab and the following year a new student joined our lab. My graduate advisor was willing to allow me to oversee many of the day-to-day research activities and training of his students, essentially letting me assume a position as "assistant coach." So during my final year at my graduate institution (now as a post-doc), I was mentoring my superstar undergraduate and four graduate students.

It was a thrilling experience to lead a team of bright scholars who were becoming more and more productive with each passing month. Although mentoring can be time-consuming, if you are working with bright, hard-working individuals it can be extremely rewarding and mutually beneficial. The productivity that can result from such synergy can be astounding!

Another reason why mentoring can drastically enhance your productivity is you can begin to delegate time-consuming tasks, such as proofreading, to your mentees. You should not feel guilty about doing so because it truly is a win-win situation. You win because you have freed up more time to pursue more specialized tasks and your mentee wins because the best way to learn how to do research is to DO research. Just remember, if you hadn't been able to actively complete these time-consuming tasks you would not have learned them yourself. However, be careful to engage in close quality control.

Extensive opportunities for mentoring are surely not common in graduate school. However, the message is you don't have to wait to become a professor to begin to have the rewarding experiences of mentoring others. If you are a professor, the message is the work you put in to mentor students is well worth it.

Chapter Summary

People are your most valuable resource for being a productive scholar. It's crucial to adopt a humble, "How can I improve?" mentality as you strive to be an outstanding apprentice. If your advisor doesn't provide critical feedback, solicit it from her. Being productive and considerate of your advisor's time will go a long way toward building a strong mentoring relationship that will maximize your productivity. Your advisor may be extremely talented, yet she is only one person. Seek additional mentorship from advanced graduate students and post-docs, your committee members, and the outside collaborators of these individuals. A senior faculty member will be helpful as you become a new professional. Don't treat mentoring as something just for new graduate students; rather, humbly try to learn all you can from as many different individuals as possible. Your productivity will see major dividends. Finally, so long as you have some experience under your belt, it's never too early to become a mentor. Investing in these efforts is sure to be rewarding both personally and professionally.

If you work hard and apply these strategies well, you will have landed an academic job before you know it. The next set of chapters describes how you can maximize principles of PEP (priorities, efficiency, and pitfall prevention) as you embark on your new career as a professor.

Chapter 15 Wrap-Up Exercises

1. Write about one or two things you found most helpful in this chapter that you want to apply to your career.

Being a Great Apprentice

2. Set up a time to meet with your advisor or a seasoned scholar whom you trust. Ask them how you may be limiting yourself. Write about their response.

3. What are some specific changes you want to make based on the feedback you received?

Seeking Mentorship

4. Make a list of three individuals from whom you could potentially receive helpful mentorship.

   Person #1_____

   Person #2_____

   Person #3_____

5. Write about your plan to receive mentorship from person #1:
6. Write about your plan to receive mentorship from person #2:
7. Write about your plan to receive mentorship from person #3:

Becoming a Mentor

8. Write down the names of one or more individuals you could potentially mentor.
9. Now, write down your plan for approaching this/these individual(s).

16 Transition Into Your First Academic Position

Main Chapter Points

- The transition to your first academic position can be lonely and isolating.
- Continue to nurture prior relationships and to reap the benefits of these collaborations.
- Proactively approach your colleagues and form new collaborative relationships.
- Delegate whatever you can.

Chapter Introduction

Dan was just beginning his new job and the transition had been extremely difficult for him. He'd always heard that you need to establish independence from your major professor, so he wasn't doing much of anything with people from graduate school. He kept waiting for his new colleagues to invite him out to lunch or to show some interest in him, but they seemed quite busy and hadn't extended the welcome he was expecting. As a result, Dan was feeling rather lonely and isolated.

> Dan wanted to get his research off to a strong start, but was finding that he wasn't getting as much done as other professors. As a graduate student he had vowed to not be the type of professor that made his students do most of the "busy work." As a result of this lack of delegation, he was doing a lot of this himself and often his students were often left out of the research process entirely.

Well, if you've made it to the professor stage, congratulations! In today's world this is an extremely impressive feat. According to the United States 2010 Census less than 1% of the population has their Ph.D. This puts you in a very exclusive group, especially when considering that fewer than 2 out of 3 of Ph.D. holders have an academic job. Well done! Now imagine that you'd like to keep your job and eventually get promoted to associate professor and gain the respect of your new colleagues. There are a number of challenges new professors face that could hinder your ability to being a productive scholar. Some of these challenges may include feeling lonely or isolated, failing to delegate, struggling to balance teaching and research, and lacking the pressure and guidance of an advisor.

Isolation

It's common for new faculty members to feel a bit lonely or isolated when they begin a new faculty appointment. You likely had developed good friendships and working relationships with individuals at your graduate institution and may find yourself missing those individuals. In addition, you may find that everyone in your new department isn't clamoring to get to know you and include you in their research. Professors are busy and it just may not be enough of a priority for them to initiate an appointment with you. Earlier we discussed the importance of synergy with mentors and collaborators as being crucial to your success in publishing, and this is why overcoming these feelings of loneliness and isolation is crucial to your productivity. Here are a few suggestions:

Don't Cut Your Old Ties, Maximize Them

A common theme in academics is the need to distance yourself from your advisor and demonstrate your independence. Although there is a need to eventually do this (you don't want to always be seen as being in your former advisor's shadow), there isn't a need to rush this process. Of course, you'll want to begin new collaborations that don't involve your former advisor, but don't hesitate to draw on your former advisor for her continued guidance and expertise. Chances are that you have incomplete projects you've begun with your advisor or other students and professors at your graduate institution. Keep these collaborative relationships strong.

Not only will you benefit tremendously from successfully completing your past work, but maintaining these relationships will help you to feel more connected and less lonely. Given that these relationships can be difficult to continue at the same level long distance, you may consider arranging a trip back to your graduate institution to be able to better nurture these collaborative ties. You could even negotiate extra startup money to do so. Again, you do want to establish some independence, but I've heard from several people that being too anxious for independence lost opportunities for them.

Proactively Approach New Colleagues

It can be a temptation when you are new to wonder why your colleagues aren't more welcoming or why they aren't inviting you to collaborate with them. Perhaps you landed in a department where you were immediately drawn into work with multiple colleagues; if so, that's great. But my hunch is that most of the time your colleagues will be busy with their own projects and may not be seeking out new collaborative ties. In many instances, if you wait for others to approach you with ideas or opportunities, you end up waiting for a long time. Why wait? Instead, be proactive and initiate contact with colleagues in your department as well as those in other departments that may share your research interests.

Perhaps a discussion of your research interests over lunch might blossom into a collaborative relationship. It's important to (a) show genuine interest in what data, resources, or expertise colleagues might possess to make them feel valued and to learn what they might bring to the table in a collaboration and to (b) make it clear how they might benefit from working with you by communicating what expertise or resources you could offer them.

You can then gauge by their reactions how interested they are in what you have to offer or if you should focus more on helping them to maximize their own resources. For instance, don't be too disappointed if they aren't very interested in the data you've collected or have access to, as their lack of familiarity with what you have may make them reluctant to invest themselves. Rather, you may need to creatively tie your interest or expertise to their data resources. Simply getting to know other faculty members on a strictly social basis will be valuable—it's always nice to have friends at work. Also, some universities have interdisciplinary centers that can be a source of potential collaborative ties.

Delegation

Some new (and not so new) professors get stuck in the trap of doing a lot of things they really shouldn't be doing. There are a lot of reasons for this. Maybe you resented your advisor in graduate school for making you do the tasks that they didn't want to do themselves. Perhaps you didn't even think of having someone else do the work, or perhaps you don't trust others to do the work to the standard you would like to see it done. Regardless of the reason, to reach your maximum levels of productivity, you've got to unburden yourself of all tasks that can reasonably be done by someone else. The most successful people in life are the ones who spend the highest percentage of their time doing things that only they can do, developing their inner genius.

Be Selective About Your Students

To be able to delegate, it's essential to have students you know you can rely on. You may feel flattered when someone wants to work with you, or you may be tempted to take on someone who isn't interested in what you are studying just for the sake of having a student. Don't get overanxious. It's important to carefully screen your future students to ensure they'll be reliable. I've personally found GPA is one of the best predictors of a good student. Some have incredible test scores and a great deal of intelligence, but you can't rely on them to get the job done. A high GPA indicates they have intelligence and work ethic. A not-so-stellar student can be a huge drag on your time and energy.

Another way of getting excellent students may be by checking into the posters at a conference poster session to find good quality research. Just the fact that they are at a conference is a good sign they are a go-getter. Additionally, you could ask colleagues at other universities to refer some of their best students to you.

There are many types of tasks in specific domains that could effectively be delegated to others. Although this may not be a comprehensive list for your domain of research, I've listed some general tasks for the areas of research and writing. I will also discuss delegation in the teaching domain in Chapter 18.

Literature Reviews

Writing a literature review can be extremely time intensive as it involves sifting through dozens or even hundreds of articles and carefully compiling them. Is this a task that a student could do under your supervision and guidance? It's helpful for them to learn these skills anyway. Of course, you'll probably want to check what they missed and go through what they wrote carefully; however, this is a task that shouldn't necessarily take your precious time. Besides turning to a student, you may consider finding a collaborator with expertise in the topic of your paper and have him write this section.

Data Collection

If you are in a field in which data is collected, you know it can be a very time intensive venture. Get students involved in the process as much as possible. Once you have a graduate student or even a capable undergraduate student with a good head, you can appoint this person to supervise the work of newer or less experienced students. This can save you a great deal of time. For instance, I initially supervised my undergraduate students myself and met with them to code video data. Once I got things rolling and they didn't need as much supervision, I pulled aside some of the more bright and trusted students and appointed them as team leaders. They were excited to have this kind of opportunity and to put it on their curriculum vitae.

Later, I appointed a capable graduate student to oversee all the team leaders and students working under each team leader. This saved me a great deal of time as this graduate student coordinated all their schedules, answered most of the everyday questions, and I'd step in with the questions the graduate student didn't know the answer to. Removing myself from the first line of fire helped save me time and develop leadership in my students.

Data Preparation and Analysis

Data preparation and analysis can be extremely time-consuming. This isn't the type of thing you can delegate right away as it needs to be done carefully and correctly. My policy now is to not do any data analysis unless I have a student sitting by my side watching and learning. This can be an effective way to teach your students how to do data analysis while you're actually doing it, knocking out two birds with one stone. As they demonstrate higher levels of proficiency, your students will be able to begin doing the analysis independently with your guided supervision. Once they are trained, they can save you a lot of time.

Reference Sections

You should never spend your time putting together a reference section or checking to see if the reference section is complete and matches all the in-text citations within the manuscript. Always make sure you are delegating this task to students, though you'll want to make sure they know what they are doing and check their work the first time.

Proofreading

Of course, you'll want to proofread articles yourself; however, this is another task you should delegate. Typos can undermine a manuscript and lead reviewers to question whether the research was also sloppy. Thus, it is helpful to not only go through the manuscript yourself, but have a couple of students or colleagues read it through for content and typos.

Chapter Summary

Making the transition to being a professor is typically not easy. You probably spent several years and developed many friendships at your graduate institution and have gone to a new place where the rules are different and you don't have strong interpersonal connections. This can lead to feeling lonely and isolated. Of course, you don't want to rely too heavily on your graduate advisor and prior connections, but don't cut off ties. Continue to nurture those prior relationships and to reap the benefits of these collaborations. Also, it's easy to feel like your new colleagues should be making efforts to get to know you and to thoroughly welcome you. But, don't wait around hoping someone makes the contact with you, rather, proactively approach your colleagues.

There are many tasks that require a lot of time and not a great deal of specialty training. These are not tasks you should be spending your precious time doing. Instead, delegate what you can and don't feel guilty about it. You are being paid for your expertise and others will learn and grow from those things you delegate to them. Don't squander your time on something that can easily and competently be done by someone else.

Successfully transitioning to your first academic position will be extremely important. However, this transition remains incomplete until you drastically increase your efficiency and ability to contribute in a meaningful way through becoming an outstanding mentor. This is the topic of the next chapter.

Chapter 16 Wrap-Up Exercises

1. Write about one or two things you found most helpful in this chapter that you want to apply to your career.

Isolation

2. What are some of your prior collaborative relationships you hope to maintain?
3. List three professors in your new department/university you would like to get to know better and your plan for connecting with them.

Delegation

4. Think about the tasks you spend time on. List out the tasks you are currently doing, which you could reasonably delegate to someone else, each on a separate line. Next to each of these tasks, write the names of one or more individuals you could have complete this task on your behalf.

17 Mentor Students and Receive Mentorship: A Professor's Guide

Main Chapter Points

- Mentoring students can be one of the most rewarding aspects of being a professor.
- Establish clear expectations for each other up front and regularly check in about how you are both living up to those expectations.
- Be authoritative and help your students know they are accountable. Give needed feedback, but in a reasonable and constructive way.
- Give practical help, teaching them how to successfully navigate the academic waters.
- Don't waste your time on those who don't have a desire to become serious scholars.
- Seek continued mentorship through the official program in your department or by requesting such mentorship from a trusted senior colleague.

Chapter Introduction

> Christian prides himself on being a good mentor. He is working with five graduate and three undergraduate students, and they all like him quite a bit. In fact, they speak glowingly about working with him to other students and faculty members. Aside from being liked by his students, Christian has helped each of them to become very productive. At first it was a lot of work and a large investment of time, but now Christian has formed leaders among the research assistants and the older ones now do a lot of the training of the younger students for him. Christian's former students have gone on to get great jobs and make strong contributions to their field. Through his students, Christian is leaving a very strong legacy.

You have successfully completed your apprenticeship—now comes the tricky part: selecting your own apprentice. This is where you must not only apply everything you've learned in the past, but also be able to teach it to others. However, don't try to go it alone; you have an entire guild of professors from whom you can select one or more people to provide guidance and help you on your new path.

Mentoring Students

Mentoring, if done right, can drastically increase your productivity. However, this is not the only reason to be involved as a mentor. Mentoring students can be one of the most enriching experiences of being an academic. Being able to play an integral role in the formation of someone's research career is truly satisfying. The term "generativity" was coined by Erik Erikson in the 1950s. It describes a concern for establishing and guiding the next generation, which precisely depicts the possibilities for mentoring. I have always felt like I received excellent mentoring and being a mentor myself was my way of paying it forward or demonstrating my gratitude for what I have received.

Aside from the satisfaction that can be gained by building the next generation of scholars, mentoring students often provides promotions and pay raises (Tenenbaum, Crosby, & Gliner, 2001). You can actually demonstrate how much value you can bring to your department as you help to produce quality students that reflect well on the university and your program.

Establish Clear Expectations for Each Other

The majority of supervisors don't explicitly state what is expected in the student-supervisor relationship. Do not simply hope your student will be able to absorb your expectations; rather, sit down and have an open discussion with your student about your expectations, perhaps even presenting it to them in writing. Being explicit will create more defined boundaries and clearer expectations of the student (Hockey, 1994). In addition, inquire from your students to know what they expect from you. What do they hope to gain from their apprenticeship with you? Learning what they want out of the relationship will help you to better cater to their needs.

Hold an occasional meeting in which you discuss how you feel your students are living up to your expectations and how you are living up to theirs. Be open to their feedback, and seek to do your best to implement their worthwhile suggestions. If you are willing to listen to them and strive to be better for them, they'll be more likely to do the same for you. Don't forget this is a two-way relationship and if you are humble enough to take feedback from your students you can grow into a truly outstanding mentor. Your humble desire to grow and improve will be refreshing for your student and perhaps even inspiring, unless your words are hollow and you make no real effort to change for the better.

For example, you could ask your student to give you a suggestion or two about something you could change or improve and, if it's reasonable, really make the effort to improve in that area.

Be Authoritative

The parenting literature describes three main types of parenting: authoritarian, permissive, and authoritative (Baumrind, 1966). As the parent of four boys, I believe many aspects of parenting apply to being a good mentor, and I will now describe how each parenting type could apply to mentoring.

Authoritarian style. This type of mentoring can be described as militant—inflexible, unbending, and harsh. This type of mentor cracks the whip and incites fear in their students. Unforgiving and even threatening, this type of advisor may get some results, but it will stem largely from extrinsic motivation and fear rather than true lasting desire from within. The students of the authoritarian professors are usually unhappy, but may be getting at least some work done. They often look with a longing eye to fellow students whose professors are permissive, not realizing this style could be even worse for students.

Permissive style. Permissive professors are the polar opposite of authoritarian professors. They want to be their students' friend, require very little, and enforce next to nothing. Perhaps they like to avoid confrontation, but they struggle to lay down the law at all. The biggest problem with this style is that many students end up floundering and accomplishing very little without someone to give them a little push. This type of professor is very pleasant to work with, but in the end, it may have been worth it to have paid your dues with the authoritarian.

Authoritative style. There is a third and final style, which unfortunately isn't as common as it should be. An authoritative style essentially is a nice combination of authoritarian and permissive. The authoritative professors will hold their student accountable, but their expectations will be reasonable, and they will not be harsh in how they follow up with a student. Students of authoritative professors will be much more likely to be intrinsically motivated and more likely to discover true excitement and passion for what they are studying because they are not impelled by fear or intimidation.

Give Practical Help

Mentorship is very similar to an apprenticeship, in which an apprentice not only learns the trade, but also learns how to navigate and succeed in the guild. Good mentors not only teach their students how to conduct and write excellent research, but will help them learn that the strategies for success involve more than simply research and writing training. Perhaps you could give your student a copy of this book or discuss the principles contained herein. As we discussed previously, it is not typically the smartest or the most gifted individuals who are the most productive, but rather it is those who employ the best strategies.

Helping your students to navigate the departmental politics is crucial to their survival. Furthermore, helping your students to tap into your own network of scholars as well as teaching them how to build their own collaborative networks is a gift that will keep giving. In fact, research has shown that giving students practical help positively influences their productivity (Tenenbaum, Crosby, & Gliner, 2001) and helps them develop competence, confidence, and effectiveness through the mentor's psychosocial help (Kram, 1983).

Don't Waste Time on Unmotivated Students

Unfortunately, there are plenty of unmotivated students out there in academia. I've seen students that seemed to show a lot of promise and potential only to end up being unmotivated. You've got to respect people's free will and your own lack of control over someone else's efforts. I think many such students realize (perhaps not even consciously) the academic lifestyle is not for them, but they are unwilling to accept the time and money they have invested as a sunken cost and change course; instead, they want to finish their degree. Perhaps they are more enamored with the title of "doctor" than they are with actually doing the research. Or perhaps they enjoy other aspects of being a professor (e.g., teaching), but didn't realize the essential role research plays in the academe and in getting a tenure-track job at any university.

Whatever the case may be, you can choose to invest a lot of time and anxiety in trying to get an unmotivated student to begin performing at a high level, or you can officially or unofficially remove the unmotivated student from your time investment bank and spend time with the students who show promise and perform. I'm not recommending you give up on someone too quickly; give them a few chances. But if they repeatedly let you down and fail to demonstrate they are trying to improve, or if they continue to exhibit a lot of the signs of lacking productivity, just let them go without the need to hurt feelings or burn bridges.

Again, let me emphasize the importance of causing the least amount of interpersonal damage as you can, as having someone dislike you never did anyone any good. Consider communicating your concerns in a delicate and constructive manner, and end by letting them know you value them as a person but just don't feel it's a good fit. It's important that you do let them know about your concerns as this feedback could be invaluable for them, but there's no need to do it in a rude or hurtful way. Venting your every frustration at them will only turn them into an enemy, whereas if done with care you could preserve a cordial relationship.

Of course, the politics and situations in the department will dictate whether you are able (at least at the present time) to let the person go officially. An official break is probably best because this person won't be a drag on your financial resources or hinder your chances to get a better student. It is also better because such unmotivated students can show a bad example for your other students and be a negative influence overall. It may be helpful to explore the option of their leaving with a terminal master's degree. That way they don't feel like they wasted their time and money, and they may be much better off having something to show for the years they spent.

Yet, if the political situation does not allow for an official drop, you can simply refrain from investing your time and resources in the person. The situation may be such that you lose money on this person and that may be out of your control, but you can usually control your time allocations. You might check with the department chair if they can be a teaching assistant so it doesn't come out of your research budget. If they are an unmotivated student, they will probably be just fine with this situation, as most unmotivated students don't like to be poked and prodded along anyway. Perhaps the best thing you can do for this unmotivated student is to direct him into a career he might find more fulfilling.

Receiving Continued Mentorship

Mentorship is crucial to productivity. Sometimes it may be easy to slip into the trap of thinking that mentorship is for graduate students and you no longer need continued mentorship. This is completely false. When you receive your Ph.D., it's not as if some wand is waved over your head and suddenly you have everything it takes to be an excellent scholar. Although you have learned a lot along the way, there is still a great deal left to learn. In fact, some of the most successful scholars have realized the importance of receiving mentorship at every stage of their career. The desire to learn all you can from others is the mark of a truly excellent human being. Often our pride gets in the way of admitting things that we don't know and stops us from asking for the needed help and guidance that will only make us better.

Many departments will have a formal program that will allow you to be mentored by a senior faculty member. Take advantage of this and do your best to learn from your mentor. If your university does not have such a program, that's okay. There's nothing to stop you from asking an admired senior colleague if they wouldn't mind mentoring you and having a regularly schedule short meeting to check in. Most colleagues would be flattered by such a request, and the majority would be willing to function in this role for you. After all, you got an academic job and have made it through the gauntlet, so they know you will be a worthwhile investment. Not only will this person's insights be important for you, but he may go to bat for you when you need it (e.g., when you're going up for tenure).

Chapter Summary

Mentoring students can be one of the most rewarding aspects of being a professor. It gives you the opportunity to be generative by building the next generation of scholars, and it can increase your pay and your productivity if done well. Establish clear expectations for each other upfront and check in about how you are both living up to these expectations on a regular basis. Be authoritative and help your students know they are accountable, and give needed feedback, but in a reasonable and constructive way. In addition to training your students about research, give practical help, teaching them how to successfully navigate the academic waters. Make sure not to waste your time on those who don't have a desire to become serious scholars. Make an official break where possible and in situations where this is not possible, discontinue giving time and energy to the relationship. Finally, seek continued mentorship through the official program in your department or by requesting such mentorship from a trusted senior colleague. This will pay long-term dividends.

Excelling as a mentor will allow you to make major contributions to the lives of students while maximizing your productive efficiency. Yet another form of working with students—in the classroom—bogs many professors down. Is it possible to actually teach better in less time and still enhance the lives of students in important ways?

Chapter 17 Wrap-Up Exercises

1. Write about one or two things you found most helpful in this chapter that you want to apply to your career.
2. Describe your expectations for each of your students.
3. What are your students' expectations for you?
4. We all have tendencies toward being authoritarian or permissive. Which style do you lean more toward? What is something you can do to be a more authoritative professor?
5. What can you do more of to help your students out with practical matters relating to your profession?
6. Which senior colleague is your faculty mentor? What are you doing to make the most of this mentored relationship?

18 Teach Better in Less Time

Main Chapter Points

- Teaching is an important task for professors, but it's also one that can consume massive quantities of research time.
- Preparation time can be reduced by borrowing and adapting PowerPoint slides and other materials from other teachers who have taught the course.
- Adding more group activities and participation questions reduces the material you need to generate and helps the students learn and digest the core principles of the class better.
- Avoid spending too much time on emails and the inconvenient requirements of taking attendance.
- If possible, arrange your schedule to avoid teaching during your peak writing and research hours.
- If you are able to have a teaching assistant, put this person to work and delegate as much as you can to him or her.
- Incorporate your research findings into your lectures.
- Involve your students in your research.

Chapter Introduction

> Melissa is a new professor who was reasonably successful during graduate school. She was on fellowship and therefore didn't have to teach much as a graduate student. However, now that she's a professor, she's finding it difficult to balance her research and teaching. She is driven to be a very conscientious teacher, so whenever she gets an email from a student she immediately drops whatever she is doing to reply. Many of these emails are in regards to missing class because Melissa has a pretty strict attendance policy. Also, she is paranoid about looking foolish in front of her students, so she spends 5–6 hours preparing for each hour of instruction, which leaves little time for her research. Despite all of this

> effort, Melissa was a bit stunned to get lower-than-expected teacher ratings; many of the students complained she was reading from her slides and she wasn't very engaging with the students. She didn't know what else she could do to improve her teaching, especially seeing how she was already spending so much time on it.

Let me begin by stating that I thoroughly enjoy teaching and consider it to be a very important priority for professors to do well. However, at the same time, I think teaching becomes one of those urgent tasks that can often gobble up research and writing time. Don't believe the common misconception that you can't be both a good teacher and a good researcher. However, to be a good researcher, you've got to be a smarter teacher and not let teaching dominate the majority of your time. You should definitely aim to be an outstanding teacher, but spending more time on something doesn't necessarily make you better at it. In fact, you may become a better teacher by spending a bit less time. Below are a few ways to improve your teaching abilities while spending less time.

Reducing Preparation Time

Even though getting up in front of a large group of students can be a daunting task, most scholars spend too much time preparing for this. There are certain things you can do to reduce the time you spend preparing for a lecture and actually increase its quality. In his study of productive scholars versus less productive scholars, Boice (1997) reported that productive scholars set limits on lecture preparation time, confining it to 10–15 hours per week. Newer and less productive faculty would spend 25 hours in teaching preparation compared to less than an hour on writing.

He goes on to point out that these more productive scholars "also excelled in student ratings and in expert ratings of their teaching, perhaps because they were less pressured to present as much lecture material and more likely to involve students as active learners" (p. 26). In another book, *Advice for New Faculty Members,* Boice (2000) suggests that most academics over-prepare for lectures and become so attached to what they have prepared that they can't adapt to the circumstances and respond to specific class needs. So what can be done to accomplish a better teaching result in less time? Here are a few helpful suggestions.

Don't Reinvent the Wheel

Unless this is a brand new course that you'll be teaching, surely someone in your department, a former colleague or someone you know, has taught the course before. Many professors are quite willing to share their slides and other class materials (e.g., tests, quizzes, assignments, etc.). If you can't find anyone who is willing to do so, try a Google search and you can probably find some decent slides. Of course, you'll want to make adaptations and make them your own (and give credit where it is due); however, building on what someone else has already put time into will free up several hours for your research pursuits. Most departments want some degree of uniformity between sections taught in the same class, so this can help with that aspect as well.

Also, students expect and prefer slides to have pictures and to be engaging; so to do this, you could spend countless hours searching for images and trying to make your content pleasing to the eye, or you could build off of the work someone else has already done, perhaps making the quality even better, and saving yourself a great amount of time. Some text books even come with videos, slides, lecture notes, etc., so you may also be on the lookout for those kinds of options.

Prepare More Group Discussion Activities/Questions and Fewer Slides

Many professors try to cover way too much material at a time. Of course, you'll probably be required to cover certain things, but do as much as you can to simplify and reduce the amount you teach. Instead, focus on teaching less material more effectively. Instead of spending endless hours preparing PowerPoint slide after slide to cover obscure principles in your field (and thus also having to refresh yourself on all of these obscure principles), focus on the core principles you want to teach. For instance, you can reduce your overall prep time by coming up with group activities that will help your students internalize the principles you are teaching. Students will welcome the break from the lecture and learn the material much better, and you won't need to prepare very many slides. In fact, I believe that students these days, who are constantly engaging in very interactive social networking, have come to expect more of this style of teaching. Similarly, asking thought-provoking questions that initiate a class discussion will help the students become more active learners and digest the material better while taking some of the strain off of you to do all the talking. For more active learning techniques that will alleviate the load of preparing lectures and help students internalize the material, visit this website: http://www.calstatela.edu/dept/chem/chem2/Active/main.htm.

Reducing Distraction and Time for Class Maintenance

Certain elements of class maintenance can be very distracting to the focus of professors, such as answering student emails, taking class attendance, and teaching during your prime research time. Also, many professors fail to fully utilize their teaching assistants in helping with their teaching tasks. The following suggestions will help you to adequately attend to class maintenance without it becoming detrimental to your scholarly productivity.

Schedule Specific Time to Address Student Emails

If you are an obsessive email checker like me, emails from students (especially if you have a large class) can distract you in a major way from your focus on research. One thing that has helped me is to create a separate email account which I give to students and to let them know when you will be checking the email. It is so much easier to knock out an entire batch of emails (many of which may be on the same topic, so you could even copy and paste your response from the previous email) than to have them trickle in one at a time, each one diverting you from your research. I typically choose to answer emails at a time of day when I'm tired and depleted because it doesn't seem to take as much exertion or energy to reply to emails as it does to do research. If you are the type of person who enjoys email, you may even make that your break (e.g., "If I can keep working on this paper until noon, then I'll check the email"). Whatever strategy you choose, it's important to limit the distractions you have while researching.

Don't Take Attendance Unless It's a University Requirement

College students should be treated like adults and should not have someone holding their hand and looking over their shoulder. They need to realize there are consequences for their actions and they will not be able to receive as high of a grade (or learn the material as thoroughly) if they do not attend class. More important for you, taking attendance can be time-consuming for two reasons: (1) You have to make sure to pass around the roll and have the attendance recorded in some way, and (2) you have to deal with all the emails and excuses for not coming to class. When I was required to take attendance as a TA, I noticed a huge influx in grandmother deaths right before and right after Thanksgiving break and Spring break. This always puts you in an uncomfortable position because you can either take them at their word, giving free points to students who don't deserve it, or you can do extensive detective work that costs you precious time and potentially insult those whose beloved grandma actually happened to die right before Spring break.

You may be concerned that not taking attendance will severely reduce the number of people who show up to your class. In this case, you may consider not posting slides and/or giving unannounced quizzes or class activities in which they turn something in for points. If you administer such quizzes, I have found it's a good policy to let them know you will drop their lowest quiz score. This way, they don't have to worry if they get sick or have a funeral to attend, and they only need to consult you if they have a major life catastrophe that makes them miss several class periods. Implementing these strategies has helped maintain good attendance in my classes while significantly reducing my hassle in dealing with emails and record keeping.

Try Not to Teach During Your Golden Research Time

If you have found you're especially productive in your research at certain times of the day, you may want to try protecting that time by discussing with your department chair (or whoever decides those things) what time of day you would prefer to teach. This is something you may not have much control over, and you may just need to accept it and do what you're told, but there's no harm in trying. In fact, you may want to point out to this person that you are trying to maximize your research productivity. This will get a much more favorable response than would a discussion of your desire to not have to be on campus for so long. You may be surprised to find out that your preference actually fits with the departmental needs.

For instance, my golden time is in the morning from about 8 to 12. I probably get about twice as much done during those hours as I do during the rest of the hours of the day combined. When I got stuck teaching a class from 8–10:30 a.m., I noticed that it shot down nearly my entire day. It was hard to get back on track and be at my optimal productivity after losing my golden hours. The following semester, I taught a class from 12:10 to 1:20 and this was perfect for me. In fact, it was ideal because it preserved my golden hours in the morning, after which I start feeling restless and in need of a little diversion and social interaction, which was then provided by teaching. This diversion actually refreshes me, giving me the energy to pursue writing and research in the afternoon. When I voiced my preference to teach in the afternoon to the teaching coordinator, I found out that most of the professors preferred to teach in the morning, so my request actually helped to balance the needs in the department. You will never know unless you ask.

Fully Utilize Teaching Assistants

A good teaching assistant (TA) is worth their weight in gold, so it's worth spending a little extra time to select the best possible person you can get, if you have a say in the matter. Some institutions have undergraduates perform these duties, in which case you could make an online application for any interested students to apply and then pick the very best applicant. If you don't have a TA for your course, discuss the possibility of getting one or of hiring someone to help out from your startup funds. If you haven't landed a job yet, discuss this as part of the negotiation process, to ensure you have the help you need.

Make sure to delegate to your TA every possible thing in the course that can reasonably be delegated. Make it your goal to not do anything that this person could do. I personally do not require my TA to attend class so they will have more free hours to grade. When I plan the due dates for assignments, I do so with my TA's schedule in mind, making sure they will have adequate time to grade everything. For instance, I never include essays or open-ended questions on my final exam or make a paper due on the last day of class, because then I would have to grade it. My TA does nearly all the grading and grade entry for the class, handles the preparation for all exam materials (e.g., preparing the scantrons), and meets with confused students who need help, referring any serious issues to me. Thus, once I have prepped a class, mostly I'm just showing up two or three times a week to teach, which opens up a great deal of time to pursue my research interests.

Use Your Teaching to Complement Your Research

Not only can teaching be done more effectively in less time, but you can use your teaching to complement your research. For instance, you can incorporate your research into your lectures and even have your students give feedback and get involved in your research ideas.

Incorporate Your Research Into Your Lectures

If you've taught the same class multiple times you may be getting a bit tired of it. Enliven the course by incorporating your research into the lectures as examples or to demonstrate a point. You may find doing so gives you a chance to develop new ideas, motivates you to write up existing results, and will make the lecture come alive for the students. If you are more excited about what you are talking about, they will be more excited, and this will show in your student ratings. Having a lecture deadline will motivate you to complete certain slides by the scheduled date of the lecture. You could even "double dip" by preparing slides for the course that you will use for a practice run before presenting the findings at an academic conference.

Get Students Involved in Your Research

I make it a point to spice up my lectures by talking about my research. Not only does this make things more interesting for your students, but it helps them to understand the role of a professor and exposes them to the research process. If you can make it relevant to the course material in some way, use the students to help you generate ideas, find subjects, or to be research subjects. One semester, I described a project I was working on (that related to the lecture for that day) and actually had them help me generate ideas for potential interview questions and exclusionary criteria for the study, and later I gave them extra credit for providing referrals for individuals who fit the study requirements. Involving them in this way was not only helpful to me, but it was also validating to them that I listened to their ideas and helped them learn more about the research process. I have often offered extra credit to my students to be involved in some of my research projects, after which we talk about it and draw lessons from it later in class.

Chapter Summary

Teaching is an important task for professors, but it is also one that can consume massive quantities of research time and distract from research as professors prepare lectures and manage their courses. Preparation time can be reduced by borrowing and adapting PowerPoint slides and other materials from other teachers who have taught the course. Also, adding more group activities and participation questions reduces the material you need to generate and helps the students better learn and digest the core principles of the class.

Avoid spending too much time on emails and the hassle and time requirements of taking attendance; replace this strategy with attendance quizzes in which you drop students' lowest score. If possible, arrange your schedule to avoid teaching during your peak writing and research hours.

If you are able to have a teaching assistant, put this person to work. Don't waste your available hours with the person on having them attend class; rather, delegate as many of the grading, recording, and even course development tasks as you can to them. It will be a better learning experience for this person and will save you a great deal of time.

Finally, teaching can complement your research as you incorporate your research findings into your lectures. Involve your students in your research—they will learn more about the process, and you will benefit from their perspectives.

As we've just discussed, teaching is one of those activities which can claim a great deal of a professor's time, preventing significant research from being accomplished. However, it can be done both better and faster by employing certain key strategies. Similarly, the next chapter describes an activity that many professors find to be incredibly time-consuming—being a reviewer—but which can also be done much more efficiently with the right techniques.

Chapter 18 Wrap-Up Exercises

1. Write about one or two things you found most helpful in this chapter that you want to apply to your career.
2. Do you have any new classes you will be teaching in the near future? If so, list two or three professors that have taught this class previously and your plan for contacting them to request materials.
3. Looking through the slides for your current class, what are some group activities you could do to better engage the students and trim down your preparation time?
4. Which suggestion(s) regarding distractions would make the biggest difference to you now (i.e., never taking attendance, setting up a separate email account for your classes, arranging for your teaching to occur at a time other than your prime research time)?
5. What is your plan to implement this suggestion(s)?
6. What are some teaching-related tasks you are doing now that could easily be delegated to a teaching assistant?
7. Describe an upcoming lecture in which you could incorporate some of your research or develop some of your research ideas to present to your class on a particular topic.
8. Write down an idea or two you have about your research that would be helpful to get some feedback or suggestions from a large group of young adults. Describe your plan to bounce this idea off your class or involve them some way in brainstorming or developing your research idea.

19 Serve as a Reviewer While Maintaining High Productivity

Main Chapter Points

- Reviewing manuscripts can help you make favorable impressions on the gatekeepers of your field.
- When you perform a review, remember to give positive feedback, be constructive, and distinguish the major from the minor flaws.
- Keep in mind what you were "hired for": to provide a critique based on your expertise, not to copyedit, fill in where the author came up short, or learn new methodologies.
- Keep your reviews brief and to the point.

Chapter Introduction

> As a new professor, Laura is just starting to get requests from different journals to be a reviewer. She wants to do it well, so she blocks out most of a day to perform a review. She carefully checks all the sources that the author cites and even looks in the database to see if there are any studies that the author didn't cover. When an author uses a statistical technique she is unfamiliar with, it takes even more of Laura's time since she feels the need to consult with a colleague who understands that analysis so she can learn how to do it herself to the point where she can give feedback on whether it was done correctly. She will often read the paper twice—once for content, and again for writing. She'll make a series of writing suggestions, picking apart many sentences and finding multiple grammar mistakes. In the end, her review is extremely thorough and extremely long, and Laura feels like this was time well spent.

Once you begin publishing several articles in a general area and become known for your work on this topic, you will likely begin to receive invitations to review manuscripts for different journals. If you are submitting several manuscripts that are being reviewed by others, it seems only right that you should perform this service to the field in return. Although performing such reviews can take time out of your research, if done right, it won't be too time intensive and can be helpful for your own productivity.

How Reviewing Can Enhance Your Productivity

There are a number of ways that reviewing manuscripts can actually enhance your productivity. For instance, it can help you to refine your skills, provide you with literature updates you may not have been aware of, allow you to make favorable impressions on the gatekeepers, and improve your chances for promotion and tenure.

Refining Your Skills

It's always much easier to poke holes in someone else's ideas and writing than your own. Critically evaluating another's work will help refine your own work and will improve your skills. You can learn from others' mistakes and enhance your critical thinking skills, which will reflect well in your own writing.

Provide Helpful Examples and Literature Updates

Conversely, a very compelling article can provide you with cutting-edge ideas, methods, and insights you may not gain from casually reading articles as part of a literature review. I have already admitted that I don't like to spend a lot of time reviewing literature; however, reviewing well-written articles on my topics helps give me a refresher on the most recent and innovative things that are being published.

Making Good Impressions on the Gatekeepers

Journal editors are the gatekeepers of scientific knowledge and publishing; in other words, these are people you'll want to impress. Therefore, when you perform a review, make sure to do a good job and submit your review in a timely fashion. I've talked to many editors, and several of them have expressed to me the difficulty of finding someone who will agree to perform a review. Many people that they contact either do not reply or decline to review. Some editors have told me this is one of the most difficult parts of the entire process. In fact, now that I'm an editor, I agree that so much time is spent just asking reviewer after reviewer until someone agrees to help out. Another big problem for editors is when people agree to perform a review but then take a great deal of time and have to be constantly reminded. Many of these reviewers will take a long time only to finally turn in a poor-quality review that isn't very informative. Thus, when you agree to do a review, and do it well and relatively quickly, you can score a lot of points with editors. It's never a bad professional strategy to be in good standing with the leaders of your field. Not to mention that such journal editors will be more open to your future submissions.

Improves Your Chances for Promotions and Tenure

Besides all of these perks, providing this kind of service to your profession will also help you in the tenure and promotion process. Although research/publishing seems to trump all other areas (at least at research-intensive universities), most universities want you to make progress in three areas: research, teaching, and service. Providing reviews can help you to look great in the "service" category. However, be sure to check with your department chair on how much reviewing counts in your favor, because some programs suggest turning down review requests and certainly you don't want reviewing to interfere too much with your sacred research time.

I would recommend making yourself a spreadsheet in which you track your work in this regard. On this tracking sheet, record the date that you received the review request and the date that you completed the review so you can keep track of how many days on average it takes you to reply. I write down the name of the journal and the topic of the article for my record. When you go up for full professor, you'll need to demonstrate you are becoming known in the field for your work, and requests to review articles on your topic is great evidence of this.

I also record the recommendation I gave and then, when I receive it, I read and record the editor's decision on the manuscript. This way I can get a sense for the degree to which my decision was on track with that of the journal editor. Furthermore, I like to read what the editor has written about how he or she reached their decision and record the degree to which my review was cited. This gives me a sense of how much the editor valued my review. If the editor makes a decision against your recommendation and doesn't cite your review much, you ought to carefully read the other person's review and the editor's rationale and try to learn as much as you can in order to write a better review in the future. Of course, this isn't always an indication that your review was no good, but you can learn about how to better critique the literature in your area by carefully reading these editorial letters.

Each year, I evaluate how many review requests I received from how many journals, calculate the average amount of time I spent on the review, and then set a goal for the next year. For instance, this past year I spent an average of 18 days per review; this upcoming year, my goal is to reduce my overall turn-around time to 10 days.

Performing a Quality Review in Less Time

The golden rule of doing unto others what you would have them do unto you definitely applies to reviewing manuscripts. Think of the reviews you liked, and this will give you some guidance. Following some of these suggestions could help you keep your time spent reviewing a manuscript to less than two hours.

Provide Some Positive Feedback

No matter how bad the article might have been, there is always at least something admirable about it. Of course, your primary role is not to pat the authors on the back; you were "hired" to be critical. However, I once had an editor tell me that he appreciated how I started my reviews with words of praise. This editor later invited me to be on the editorial board of his journal. It never hurts to be kind, and I'm sure you have appreciated any kind words reviewers have thrown your way, even if the overall review was negative.

Be Constructive in Your Criticism

You can get your critical points across in a way that is helpful and not destructive. Remember, this could be a student who is submitting his or her first paper, and you don't want to instill in them fear and disgust of the review process. Don't hold back critiques you have come up with just to be nice, but be sure to communicate in a constructive manner. Rather than writing what you may be thinking ("This was one of the worst manuscripts I have ever read"), consider a more constructive, "There were several aspects of the paper that could be improved." It may require some self-restraint, but it's always worth it to not hurt someone's feeling of self-worth.

Differentiate Between Minor Concerns and Fatal Flaws

Don't make the editor try to guess at what you think a minor infraction or a serious concern is; be explicit about it. I typically begin a review with some praise and then list out my major concerns followed by my minor concerns. Now, as an editor, I see that this type of format is very helpful as it helps us to more quickly make a decision on the quality of a manuscript. It makes it clear what can be fixed and what is simply unsalvageable.

You're Not a Copy Editor

One important key in performing a good review is to add value and do a nice job without the experience robbing you of too much precious research and writing time. I once had a colleague who felt she needed to spend several long hours to do an adequate job. Remember the manuscript will undergo scrutiny regarding grammar, spelling, etc., and your job is not to be a copy editor. You have been "hired" for this job because you have expertise that is valued, so share it. You can just say, "There are several typos," and perhaps point out a few examples you noted to give some guidance.

Don't Do the Author's Work

Some reviewers feel the need to do the work for the authors. For instance, don't feel like you need to take time away from your research to complete the authors' insufficient literature review or to restructure the authors' arguments for them. Furthermore, don't waste time learning the intricacies of the authors' statistical analysis, unless you want to use it yourself. If the analysis is complex, the chances are good that the editor also found a reviewer whose expertise lends itself to this particular type of analysis. If you feel it could be an issue, be humble enough to let an editor know you are unfamiliar with the analysis and therefore cannot give judgment on that portion of the manuscript. However, the editor probably contacted you for your topical expertise, so it shouldn't be a big deal. Again, unless you want to use that method or statistical tool, it's not worth your time to try to learn it.

Keep It Brief

I have had reviews that have filled more than 8 single-spaced pages, making my cover letter submitted with revisions over 20 pages long. That's almost an entire manuscript length just replying to reviewer concerns. I imagine you aren't thrilled when you see a very long review, and neither is the author on the receiving end. Also, as an editor I do not like to have to trudge through such a long review, especially when it is clear the article needs to be rejected. You'll not only save yourself a great deal of time by keeping your responses succinct, but you'll also make everyone else happy. You want to provide sufficient information, but you can be relatively thorough and brief with much less effort.

Chapter Summary

Being an outstanding reviewer while maintaining high levels of productivity is definitely a balancing act. Reviewing manuscripts can help you make favorable impressions on the gatekeepers of your field. When you do a review, give positive feedback, be constructive, and distinguish the major from the minor flaws. To save time as you complete your review, remember what you were "hired for"—to provide a critique based on your expertise. This will help you to refrain from copyediting, filling in author gaps, trying to learn new methods, and waxing long. Serving the field as a reviewer doesn't have to take away from your productivity; if done correctly, it can enhance it.

Chapter 19 Wrap-Up Exercises

1. Write about one or two things you learned from this chapter that could help you in your career.
2. What are some things you could change to improve the quality and speed of your reviews?
3. Think about the reviews you have already completed and estimate how long it took you from the time you got the manuscript to the time you submitted your review. Now come up with a goal to decrease the amount of time it will take you for current and future reviews and a plan for how you will do that.

20 Conclusion
Putting It All Together

Congratulations! If you are reading this chapter, you probably have read all or most of the book. Unfortunately, the majority of book buyers never make it to the end, so you are part of an elite group. We've covered a lot of material, and hopefully you've gained some insights and strategies that will increase the academic prosperity in your life. I truly believe that increasing your productivity will greatly improve your chances of graduating with distinction and being attractive to employers; you not only won't worry about tenure but will look forward to it; you will get raises and promotions; you will be the recipient of admiration, respect, and freedom; and you will be generative and make important contributions to your field, colleagues, and students. This is all in addition to the sheer sense of satisfaction that comes from excelling in one's career. Of course, there are no guarantees in life; however, learning and living the principles of enhanced productivity is the most likely way to ensure prosperity in academia.

You can achieve academic prosperity by applying PEP principles of priorities, efficiency, and prevention. Regarding priorities, I discussed how we need to put first things first by making research both important and urgent (Chapter 1). The importance of research can be enhanced by choosing a topic you feel passionate about (Chapter 2), and the urgency of your research can be strengthened through goals (Chapter 3) and by delighting in deadlines (Chapter 4).

You can speed up and improve your writing by applying the suggestions in Chapter 5. Efficiency can be improved by beginning several projects at different stages to both increase your total number of manuscripts and decrease waiting time for collaborators and reviewers (Chapter 6). A great deal of wasted time can be eliminated by applying the hot potato principle and getting the ball (manuscript) out of your court as quickly as you can (Chapter 7). Finally, create multiple streams of passive income (publications) by teaming up with other scholars (Chapter 8). This teamwork will help you improve your work even as you spend less time on it.

Remember, all of these strategies will be for naught if you don't take preventative action against the many pitfalls that commonly beset the best-intentioned researcher. Among these pitfalls are those that come from inside yourself: the five enemies from within (Chapter 9) and burnout (Chapter 10). However, there are equally harmful foes that come from without that you must ward off in order to ensure your prosperity, including distractions (Chapter 11) and rejection (Chapter 12).

Finally, there are some specific ways to enhance academic prosperity at different stages in your career. Given that students will one day become professors, and professors usually mentor students, these strategies should be helpful for all readers. Chapter 13 documented how undergraduates may apply principles of PEP. I also discussed how graduate students can make the transition from a student mentality to a professional mentality (Chapter 14) and how they can be better mentees and mentors (Chapter 15). If you are already a professor or you just became one, review Chapter 16 on maintaining productivity during and after the transition to becoming a professor. New professionals should also review Chapter 17 to improve on bringing out the best in your students, Chapter 18 to learn to teach better in less time, and Chapter 19 for tips on being a good reviewer while maintaining high levels of productivity, all of which increase your overall efficiency.

Now you have learned how to create a future filled with academic prosperity by applying the principles of priorities, efficiency, and prevention. In other words, you have learned to build your PEP mansion! If you haven't yet completed the self-assessment in Appendix A, I recommend you do so in order to see where you are at and what you need to improve on the most. I sincerely hope the approaches and strategies I have described will be helpful to you in building a successful and productive career. You will undoubtedly gain knowledge about specific aspects of the writing process from other sources. However, having read this book, you now have the keys to successful building approaches and strategies that will guide you in your quest for significant achievements. Move forward and unlock your full potential, then pay it forward by teaching someone else to do the same. I wish you the best in the extremely gratifying journey that awaits you!

Appendix A
Determining Your Strengths and Weaknesses: A Professional Self-Assessment

Becoming acquainted with your strengths and weaknesses is the first brick to be laid on the path to ultimate productivity. It is important to gain a clear understanding of your professional self. I recommend you carefully read and reread each chapter in this book; however, this appendix will identify some specific chapters you may want to concentrate on.

In this section, I'm going to ask a series of questions you should answer as truthfully as you possibly can. I also suggest you revisit the questions in this chapter at the conclusion of each academic year so you can mark your progress in each domain and set goals for further improvement. If you are just beginning your graduate school career, some of the questions may not apply to you; if this is the case, simply write N/A in the left column. Now, go ahead and get started!

Chapter 1

1. I spend more than half my time on classes or teaching.

   1 2 3 4 5 6 7 8 9 10
   Strongly disagree   Strongly agree

2. I get nervous and uptight when thinking about having my work reviewed.

   1 2 3 4 5 6 7 8 9 10
   Strongly disagree   Strongly agree

3. Research may be important for me, but honestly it's not very urgent.

   1 2 3 4 5 6 7 8 9 10
   Strongly disagree   Strongly agree

4. I don't have a specific time and place set aside for writing.

   1 2 3 4 5 6 7 8 9 10
   Strongly disagree   Strongly agree

   Sum of all question ratings ____

148 Appendix A

Chapter 2

1. I'm having a difficult time choosing what I want to study.

   1   2   3   4   5   6   7   8   9   10
   Strongly disagree   Strongly agree

2. I don't really enjoy the topic I'm researching.

   1   2   3   4   5   6   7   8   9   10
   Strongly disagree   Strongly agree

3. Usually, someone else chooses my research topic for me.

   1   2   3   4   5   6   7   8   9   10
   Strongly disagree   Strongly agree

4. I do research on multiple different topics.

   1   2   3   4   5   6   7   8   9   10
   Strongly disagree   Strongly agree

   Sum of all question ratings ____

Chapter 3

1. I don't typically set goals.

   1   2   3   4   5   6   7   8   9   10
   Strongly disagree   Strongly agree

2. I have a hard time evaluating good goals for myself that I can reach.

   1   2   3   4   5   6   7   8   9   10
   Strongly disagree   Strongly agree

3. I never work toward a group goal.

   1   2   3   4   5   6   7   8   9   10
   Strongly disagree   Strongly agree

4. I don't feel accountable to someone else for my goals.

   1   2   3   4   5   6   7   8   9   10
   Strongly disagree   Strongly agree

   Sum of all question ratings ____

Chapter 4

1. I haven't used my course papers very often as the start of a publishable manuscript.

   1   2   3   4   5   6   7   8   9   10
   Strongly disagree   Strongly agree

2. I usually submit well-developed research to a conference so I don't have to do much extra work to get it ready.

   1   2   3   4   5   6   7   8   9   10
   Strongly disagree   Strongly agree

3. I don't like to promise that I'm going to deliver something by a set date.

   1   2   3   4   5   6   7   8   9   10
   Strongly disagree   Strongly agree

4. I don't usually use deadlines as a way to motivate myself.

   1   2   3   4   5   6   7   8   9   10
   Strongly disagree   Strongly agree

   Sum of all question ratings ____

Chapter 5

1. I tend to review all of the literature I can find about a topic before I begin writing.

   1   2   3   4   5   6   7   8   9   10
   Strongly disagree   Strongly agree

2. My manuscripts tend to be on the longer side.

   1   2   3   4   5   6   7   8   9   10
   Strongly disagree   Strongly agree

3. I try to make my writing sound very elevated and sophisticated.

   1   2   3   4   5   6   7   8   9   10
   Strongly disagree   Strongly agree

4. I don't have a set strategy for outlining or organizing my ideas before I begin writing.

   1   2   3   4   5   6   7   8   9   10
   Strongly disagree   Strongly agree

   Sum of all question ratings ____

Chapter 6

1. I typically focus on one project at a time.

   1   2   3   4   5   6   7   8   9   10
   Strongly disagree   Strongly agree

2. I don't have a system in place for tracking my progress on my research projects.

   1   2   3   4   5   6   7   8   9   10
   Strongly disagree   Strongly agree

3. I often find myself wondering what to do next with my research as I wait for my advisor to give me feedback or for my data to be collected.

   1   2   3   4   5   6   7   8   9   10
   Strongly disagree   Strongly agree

4. I typically get one project completed before beginning another.

   1   2   3   4   5   6   7   8   9   10
   Strongly disagree   Strongly agree

   Sum of all question ratings ____

Chapter 7

1. When I receive a manuscript from a coauthor, it usually takes me quite a while to reply with feedback.

   1   2   3   4   5   6   7   8   9   10
   Strongly agree   Strongly disagree

2. When I receive a "revise and resubmit" decision from a journal on a manuscript, it usually takes me quite a while to get around to fixing it up.

   1   2   3   4   5   6   7   8   9   10
   Strongly agree   Strongly disagree

3. When my manuscript is rejected, it usually takes me quite a while to resubmit.

   1   2   3   4   5   6   7   8   9   10
   Strongly disagree   Strongly agree

4. When I get a manuscript I've worked on back from others revising it, I put off opening it up again and hashing through the comments.

   1   2   3   4   5   6   7   8   9   10
   Strongly disagree   Strongly agree

   Sum of all question ratings ____

Chapter 8

1. I'm rarely on the lookout for high-quality collaborators.

   1   2   3   4   5   6   7   8   9   10
   Strongly disagree   Strongly agree

2. I am a bit slow at responding to a collaborator with feedback on a manuscript.

   1   2   3   4   5   6   7   8   9   10
   Strongly disagree   Strongly agree

3. I typically do not tell people what I actually think about their work for fear of hurting their feelings.

   1   2   3   4   5   6   7   8   9   10
   Strongly disagree   Strongly agree

4. I'm not actively building any new skills that could be helpful in attracting others to collaborate with me.

   1   2   3   4   5   6   7   8   9   10
   Strongly disagree   Strongly agree

   Sum of all question ratings ____

Chapter 9

1. I tend to procrastinate research tasks.

   1   2   3   4   5   6   7   8   9   10
   Strongly disagree   Strongly agree

2. Many people consider me to be a bit of a perfectionist.

   1 2 3 4 5 6 7 8 9 10
   Strongly disagree   Strongly agree

3. To get something published, I think it should be groundbreaking.

   1 2 3 4 5 6 7 8 9 10
   Strongly disagree   Strongly agree

4. I spend a high proportion of my "research time" reading the literature in my field.

   1 2 3 4 5 6 7 8 9 10
   Strongly disagree   Strongly agree

   Sum of all question ratings ____

Chapter 10

1. My life is out of balance.

   1 2 3 4 5 6 7 8 9 10
   Strongly disagree   Strongly agree

2. I could definitely use more exercise.

   1 2 3 4 5 6 7 8 9 10
   Strongly disagree   Strongly agree

3. People I'm close to often complain that I'm not spending very much time with them.

   1 2 3 4 5 6 7 8 9 10
   Strongly disagree   Strongly agree

4. I get so caught up in my next endeavor that I don't actually take the time to fully celebrate my achievements.

   1 2 3 4 5 6 7 8 9 10
   Strongly disagree   Strongly agree

   Sum of all question ratings ____

Chapter 11

1. I often check my texts or social media (e.g., Twitter and Facebook) while I am writing or doing research tasks.

   1　2　3　4　5　6　7　8　9　10
   Strongly disagree　　　　　　　　　　　Strongly agree

2. I rarely reach the state of flow (complete focus and immersion in a task).

   1　2　3　4　5　6　7　8　9　10
   Strongly disagree　　　　　　　　　　　Strongly agree

3. I spend a lot of time shooting the breeze with fellow students or colleagues.

   1　2　3　4　5　6　7　8　9　10
   Strongly disagree　　　　　　　　　　　Strongly agree

4. I have my email open all the time and when I get an email I read it immediately regardless of what I'm working on.

   1　2　3　4　5　6　7　8　9　10
   Strongly disagree　　　　　　　　　　　Strongly agree

   Sum of all question ratings ____

Chapter 12

1. Fear of rejection often hinders me from submitting my work for publication.

   1　2　3　4　5　6　7　8　9　10
   Strongly disagree　　　　　　　　　　　Strongly agree

2. When one article is rejected, I find it very hard to submit it again to another journal for fear of getting rejected again.

   1　2　3　4　5　6　7　8　9　10
   Strongly disagree　　　　　　　　　　　Strongly agree

3. I believe the best scholars in the field rarely have their work rejected.

   1　2　3　4　5　6　7　8　9　10
   Strongly disagree　　　　　　　　　　　Strongly agree

4. When I read rejection letters from reviewers, I often get angry or upset.

   1   2   3   4   5   6   7   8   9   10
   Strongly disagree   Strongly agree

                         Sum of all question ratings ____

Chapter 13

1. I have actively pursued research opportunities with professors in the field I have chosen.

   1   2   3   4   5   6   7   8   9   10
   Strongly disagree   Strongly agree

2. I'm picking a graduate program based more on the quality of the program than on the quality of an individual faculty member I'm interested in working with.

   1   2   3   4   5   6   7   8   9   10
   Strongly disagree   Strongly agree

3. I think doing practice tests for the GRE is a waste of time.

   1   2   3   4   5   6   7   8   9   10
   Strongly disagree   Strongly agree

4. I don't plan to contact the professors I'm interested in working with to find out if they're taking students.

   1   2   3   4   5   6   7   8   9   10
   Strongly disagree   Strongly agree

                         Sum of all question ratings ____

Chapter 14

1. I experience a great deal of anxiety about getting good grades in my graduate classes.

   1   2   3   4   5   6   7   8   9   10
   Strongly disagree   Strongly agree

2. I tend to get my class assignments done before tackling research projects.

   | 1 | 2 | 3 | 4 | 5 | 6 | 7 | 8 | 9 | 10 |

   Strongly disagree   Strongly agree

3. Times when classes are out, like between semesters or during the summer, are a nice and needed respite from academic work.

   1   2   3   4   5   6   7   8   9   10

   Strongly disagree   Strongly agree

4. My Master's thesis/Dissertation is what matters most to me during graduate school.

   1   2   3   4   5   6   7   8   9   10

   Strongly disagree   Strongly agree

   Sum of all question ratings ____

Chapter 15

1. I find it difficult to ask for feedback, especially from people who have authority over me.

   1   2   3   4   5   6   7   8   9   10

   Strongly disagree   Strongly agree

2. The only person I collaborate with is my major professor.

   1   2   3   4   5   6   7   8   9   10

   Strongly disagree   Strongly agree

3. I don't think it's appropriate for graduate students to seek mentorship from someone other than their major professor.

   1   2   3   4   5   6   7   8   9   10

   Strongly disagree   Strongly agree

4. I haven't seriously considered mentoring undergraduate students or fellow graduate students.

   1   2   3   4   5   6   7   8   9   10

   Strongly disagree   Strongly agree

   Sum of all question ratings ____

Chapter 16

1. I have heard you should establish independence from your graduate mentor, so I don't collaborate with him or her much at all anymore.

    1　　2　　3　　4　　5　　6　　7　　8　　9　　10
    Strongly disagree　　　　　　　　　　　　　　Strongly agree

2. I think my new colleagues should be reaching out to me more often.

    1　　2　　3　　4　　5　　6　　7　　8　　9　　10
    Strongly disagree　　　　　　　　　　　　　　Strongly agree

3. I do not proactively pursue new collaborations.

    1　　2　　3　　4　　5　　6　　7　　8　　9　　10
    Strongly disagree　　　　　　　　　　　　　　Strongly agree

4. I don't like delegating tasks to others.

    1　　2　　3　　4　　5　　6　　7　　8　　9　　10
    Strongly disagree　　　　　　　　　　　　　　Strongly agree

    Sum of all question ratings _____

Chapter 17

1. I don't actually talk with my students about what I expect from them and what they expect from me.

    1　　2　　3　　4　　5　　6　　7　　8　　9　　10
    Strongly disagree　　　　　　　　　　　　　　Strongly agree

2. I focus exclusively on writing and research and don't talk to my students about how they can navigate the academic waters.

    1　　2　　3　　4　　5　　6　　7　　8　　9　　10
    Strongly disagree　　　　　　　　　　　　　　Strongly agree

3. I spend a lot of time trying to motivate students who don't seem to be into the research.

    1　　2　　3　　4　　5　　6　　7　　8　　9　　10
    Strongly disagree　　　　　　　　　　　　　　Strongly agree

Appendix A 157

4. Now that I'm a faculty member, I don't really need mentoring anymore.

   1   2   3   4   5   6   7   8   9   10
   Strongly disagree   Strongly agree

   Sum of all question ratings ____

Chapter 18

1. I create all my slides, tests, assignments, etc., from scratch.

   1   2   3   4   5   6   7   8   9   10
   Strongly disagree   Strongly agree

2. My focus is on lecturing and I rarely, if ever, have the students do interactive group work.

   1   2   3   4   5   6   7   8   9   10
   Strongly disagree   Strongly agree

3. I often end up teaching during my best research and writing hours.

   1   2   3   4   5   6   7   8   9   10
   Strongly disagree   Strongly agree

4. My teaching assistant often doesn't have enough to do to fill her assigned hours.

   1   2   3   4   5   6   7   8   9   10
   Strongly disagree   Strongly agree

   Sum of all question ratings ____

Chapter 19

1. I often spend an entire day reviewing a manuscript.

   1   2   3   4   5   6   7   8   9   10
   Strongly disagree   Strongly agree

2. I often find myself giving extensive writing suggestions and fixing multiple grammar mistakes.

   1   2   3   4   5   6   7   8   9   10
   Strongly disagree   Strongly agree

3. I sometimes will learn a lot about a method that is not relevant to my work so that I can adequately evaluate an article.

   1 2 3 4 5 6 7 8 9 10
   Strongly disagree   Strongly agree

4. I don't think reviewing manuscripts is worth my time.

   1 2 3 4 5 6 7 8 9 10
   Strongly disagree   Strongly agree

   Sum of all question ratings ____

Interpreting Your Scores

You may have noticed all the questions are worded such that higher scores indicate greater need for improvement in each area, and they have been arranged by chapter. Each score is out of 40. A score of 4–13 means you are in pretty good or excellent shape, 14–23 means that slight improvement is needed, 24–34 means a moderate need for improvement, and 35–40 means you have strong need for improvement in this area. Scores may vary for each chapter, so, for example, if you find your scores tend to be higher under the Chapter 2 questions, you will want to pay especially close attention to that chapter. Now glance through each of the chapter questions and report the three chapters that appear to have the highest scores.

Highest Score Chapter _____
Second Highest Score Chapter _____
Third Highest Score Chapter _____

While each chapter is relevant and contains information that will be helpful, you will want to pay special attention to the chapters you listed above as these are areas you will benefit the most from improving. I recommend completing this assessment multiple times to track your improvement. I wish you the best as you begin this exciting journey of maximizing your effectiveness and productivity to launch yourself into a successful academic career!

Appendix B
Time Diary

Instructions: Briefly record what you did with your time for each 15 minute interval.

Date_____
7:00–7:15:_____
7:15–7:30:_____
7:30–7:45:_____
7:45–8:00:_____
8:00–8:15:_____
8:15–8:30:_____
8:30–8:45:_____
8:45–9:00:_____
9:00–9:15:_____
9:15–9:30:_____
9:30–9:45:_____
9:45–10:00:_____
10:00–10:15:_____
10:15–10:30:_____
10:30–10:45:_____
10:45–11:00:_____
11:00–11:15:_____
11:15–11:30:_____
11:30–11:45:_____
11:45–12:00:_____
12:00–12:15:_____
12:15–12:30:_____
12:30–12:45:_____
12:45–1:00:_____
1:00–1:15:_____
1:15–1:30:_____
1:30–1:45:_____
1:45–2:00:_____
2:00–2:15:_____

2:15–2:30: _____
2:30–2:45: _____
2:45–3:00: _____
3:00–3:15: _____
3:15–3:30: _____
3:30–3:45: _____
3:45–4:00: _____
4:00–4:15: _____
4:15–4:30: _____
4:30–4:45: _____
4:45–5:00: _____
5:00–5:15: _____
5:15–5:30: _____
5:30–5:45: _____
5:45–6:00: _____
6:00–6:15: _____
6:15–6:30: _____
6:30–6:45: _____
6:45–7:00: _____
7:00–7:15: _____
7:15–7:30: _____
7:30–7:45: _____
7:45–8:00: _____
8:00–8:15: _____
8:15–8:30: _____
8:30–8:45: _____
8:45–9:00: _____
9:00–9:15: _____
9:15–9:30: _____
9:30–9:45: _____
9:45–10:00: _____
10:00–10:15: _____
10:15–10:30: _____
10:30–10:45: _____
10:45–11:00: _____
11:00–11:15: _____
11:15–11:30: _____
11:30–11:45: _____
11:45–12:00: _____

Appendix C
Recommended Further Reading

Bolker, J. (1998). Your Dissertation in 15 Minutes a Day: A Guide to Starting, Revising, and Finishing Your Doctoral Thesis. New York: Owl Books.

Boice, R. (1989). Procrastination, busyness and bingeing. *Behavior Research Therapy*, *27*(6), 605–611.

Boice, R. (1994). *How writers journey to comfort and fluency: A psychological adventure*. Westport, CT: Praeger.

Boice, R. (1997). Strategies for enhancing scholarly productivity. In J. M. Moxley & T. Taylor (Eds.), *Writing and publishing for academic authors* (2nd ed., pp. 19–34). Lanham, MD: Rowman & Littlefield Publishers.

Booth, W. C., Colomb, G. G., & Williams, J. M. *The craft of research.* (2nd ed.). Chicago: The University of Chicago Press.

Darley, J. M., Zanna, M. P., Roediger, H. L., III (Eds.), The complete academic: A career guide (2nd ed.) (pp. 3–15). Washington, DC: American Psychological Association.

Feibelman P. (2011). A PhD is Not Enough: Guide to Survival in Science. New York: Basic Books.

Gray, P. & Drew., D.E. (2008). What They Didn't Teach You in Graduate School 199 Helpful Hints for Success in your Academic Career. Sterling, VA: Stylus Publishing.

Gray, T. (2010). *Publish & flourish*: *Become a prolific scholar*. Las Cruces: Teaching Academy, New Mexico State University.

Kelsky, K. L. (2013, May 30). The Professor is in. [Web Log Comment]. Retrieved from http://www.theprofessorisin.com

Kelsky, K. L. (2013, May 30). Pearls of Wisdom—The Blog. [Web Log Comment]. Retrieved from http://www.theprofessorisin.com/pearlsofwisdom

Martin, B. (2011). *Doing good things better*. Nössemark, Sweden: Irene Publishing.

O'Hanlon, B. (2007). *Write is a verb. Sit down. Start writing. No excuses.* Cincinnati, OH: Writer's Digest Books.

Reis, R. M. (1997). *Tomorrow's Professor: Preparing for Careers in Science and Engineering*. New York, NY: Computer Society Press.

Silvia, P. J. (2007). *How to write a lot: A practical guide to productive academic writing.* Washington, DC: American Psychological Association.

References

Association of Learned and Professional Society Publishers. (2000). Current practice in peer review: Results of a survey conducted during Oct/Nov 2000. Retrieved from http://www.alpsp.org.www.alpsp.org

Baumrind, D. (1966). Effects of authoritative parental control on child behavior. *Child Development, 37*(4), 887–907.

Boice, R. (1989). Procrastination, busyness and bingeing. *Behavior Research Therapy, 27*(6), 605–611.

Boice, R. (1997). Strategies for enhancing scholarly productivity. In J. M. Moxley, & T. Taylor (Eds.), *Writing and publishing for academic authors* (2nd ed., pp. 19–34). Lanham, MD: Rowman & Littlefield Publishers.

Boice, R. (2000). *Advice for new faculty members: Nihil nimus*. Needham Heights, MA: Allyn & Bacon.

Canfield, J. (2005). *The success principles*. New York: HarperCollins Publishers.

Covey, S. R. (1989). *The 7 habits of highly effective people: Powerful lessons in personal change*. New York: Simon and Schuster.

Csíkszentmihályi, M. (1998). *Finding flow: The psychology of engagement with everyday life*. New York: Basic Books.

Elbow, P. (1973/1998). *Writers without teachers*. London: Oxford University Press.

Fiske, D.W., & Fogg, L. (1990). But the reviewers are making different criticisms of my paper! Diversity and uniqueness in reviewer comments. *American Psychologist, 45*, 591–598.

Gessner, G. C., Jaggars, D. E., Rutner, J., & Tancheva, K. (2011). Supporting humanities doctoral student success: A collaborative project between Cornell University Library and Columbia University Libraries. Council on Library and Information Resources. http://www.clir.org/pubs/ruminations/02cornellcolumbia

Gray, T. (2010). *Publish & flourish: Become a prolific scholar*. Las Cruces: Teaching Academy, New Mexico State University.

Hall, S. A. & Wilcox, A. J. (2007). The fate of epidemiologic manuscripts: A study of papers submitted to *Epidemiology*. *Epidemiology, 18*, 262–265.

Hamilton, J. (2008). Think you're multitasking? Think again. Retrieved from http://www.npr.org/templates/story/story.php?storyId=95256794

Hockey, J. (1994). Establishing boundaries: Problems and solutions in managing the Ph.D. supervisor's role. *Cambridge Journal of Education, 24*, 293–305.

Kleingeld, A., van Mierlo, H., & Arends, L. (2011). The effect of goal setting on group performance: A meta-analysis. *Journal of Applied Psychology, 96*(6), 1289–1304.

Kram, K. E. (1983). Phases of the mentor relationship. *Academy of Management Journal, 26,* 608–625.

Kuhn, Thomas S. (1962). *The structure of scientific revolutions* (1st ed.). Chicago: University of Chicago Press.

Lord, C. G. (2004). A guide to PhD graduate school: How they keep score in the big leagues. In Darley, J. M., Zanna, M. P., Roediger, H. L., III (Eds.), The complete academic: A career guide (2nd ed.) (pp. 3–15). Washington, DC: American Psychological Association.

Martin, B. (2011). *Doing good things better.* Nössemark, Sweden 1: Irene Publishing.

Mills, C. W. (1959/1976). *The Sociological imagination.* New York: Oxford University Press.

O'Hanlon, B. (2007). *Write is a verb. Sit down. Start writing. No excuses.* Cincinnati, OH: Writer's Digest Books.

Ritchel, M. (2010). Growing up digital, wired for distraction. *New York Times.* Retrieved from http://www.nytimes.com/2010/11/21/technology/21brain.html?pagewanted=all

Robbins, A. (1986). *Unlimited power: The new science of personal achievement.* New York: Simon & Schuster.

Salmon, P. (2001). Effects of physical exercise on anxiety, depression, and sensitivity to stress: A unifying theory. *Clinical Psychological Review, 21,* 33–61.

Shoda, Y., Mischel, W., & Peake, P. K. (1990). Predicting adolescent cognitive and social competence from preschool delay of gratification: Identifying diagnostic conditions. *Developmental Psychology, 26,* 978–986.

Shontell, A. (2010). 80% hate their jobs—but should you choose a passion or a paycheck? Retrieved from http://articles.businessinsider.com/2010–10–04/strategy/30001895_1_new-job-passion-careers

Silvia, P. J. (2007). *How to write a lot: A practical guide to productive academic writing.* Washington, DC: American Psychological Association.

Tenenbaum, H. R., Crosby, F. J., & Gliner, M. D. (2001). Mentoring relationships in graduate school. *Journal of Vocational Behavior, 59,* 326–341.

Watkins, P. C., Cruz, L., Holben, H., & Kolts, R. L. (2008). Taking care of business? Grateful processing of unpleasant memories. *The Journal of Positive Psychology, 3,* 87–99.

Index

academic i, x, xv, xvi–xx, 4–7, 11, 29, 32, 34, 55, 56, 65, 66, 69, 71, 83, 88, 89, 91, 108, 114, 118, 120, 121, 123, 124, 127, 129, 130, 131, 133, 137, 144, 145, 147, 155, 156, 158
academic conferences 66, 71, 137
academic positions 120, 124
accountability xxi, 3, 10, 11, 19, 21, 22, 23, 25, 26, 27, 53, 67, 126, 128, 130, 148
acting as if 20
activities 6, 7, 10, 66, 69, 71, 76, 78, 117, 132, 134, 135, 137, 138
admiration xv, xvii, xviii, 115, 116, 130, 141, 144
advanced fellow students 115
advising undergraduates 86, 93, 94, 98, 99
advisor xv, xvii, 11, 13, 14, 17, 18, 19, 22, 26, 27, 38, 44, 45, 47, 57, 58, 59, 80, 84, 85, 86, 93, 94, 97, 98, 99, 103, 107, 109, 112–15, 116, 118, 120, 121, 122, 124, 128, 150
anxiety xvi, xviii, 85, 106, 107, 129, 154
apprentice 94, 103, 104, 108, 110, 112, 113, 114, 117, 118, 126, 127, 128
authoritarian 127, 128, 131
authoritative 126, 127, 128, 130, 131

balanced life ix, xxi, 56, 65, 66, 68, 70, 71, 73, 79, 86, 108, 132, 152
becoming a mentor 112, 116, 119
burnout xxi, 56, 64, 65, 72, 144

celebrating victories 65, 72, 73, 74
class maintenance 134
class prioritizer 8, 9

class projects 25, 26, 27
collaborate 47, 49, 52, 53, 121, 151, 156
collaborators xxi, 38, 43, 44, 45, 47, 48, 49, 50, 51, 52, 53, 54, 59, 72, 74, 75, 112, 115, 116, 118, 121, 144, 151
colleagues x, xi, xviii, xix, 22, 47, 49, 51, 53, 54, 62, 70, 75, 80, 81, 83, 101, 107, 120, 121, 122, 124, 130, 144, 153, 156
committee members 47, 112, 115, 118
commuting by bike 67
conference proposals 25, 26, 27, 28
conference travel 71, 72
considerate 114, 118
constructive criticism 51, 52
continued mentorship 126, 130, 131
contribution i, xv, xvii, xviii, xix, 22, 33, 52, 53, 96, 115, 126, 131, 144
copy editor 142
counterproductive 108
creating deadlines xxi, 11, 23, 25, 27, 28
criticism 3, 7, 50, 51, 52, 84, 113, 142
current events 69
cynic xxi, 57, 58, 62, 64

data analysis 13, 15, 37, 40, 123
data preparation 123
deadlines xxi, 2, 3, 10, 11, 12, 21, 23, 25, 26, 27, 28, 52, 57, 114, 137, 144, 149
delegation 64, 117, 120, 122, 123, 124, 125, 132, 136, 138, 156
difficult classes 3, 93, 96, 100, 101, 102
distractions xxi, 3, 6, 11, 56, 75, 76, 77, 78, 79, 80, 81, 108, 134, 135, 138, 145
double dipping 26, 39, 137

efficiency x, xvi, xix, xx, xxi, 27, 28, 29, 36, 37, 41, 42, 43, 46, 48, 55, 66, 89, 91, 118, 124, 131, 144, 145
eliminating wasted time 42, 144
email 6, 11, 22, 45, 48, 52, 75, 76, 78, 79, 80, 98, 99, 100, 102, 132, 134, 135, 137, 138, 153
emotional separation 39, 45, 82, 83, 86, 90
enemies from within xxi, 56, 57, 58, 64, 73, 144
expectations x, 14, 20, 47, 61, 78, 80, 109, 120, 126, 127, 128, 130, 131, 132, 134, 156
experience i, ix, x, xv, xvii, xix, 20, 39, 48, 70, 71, 72, 73, 76, 81, 82, 83, 85, 94, 95, 103, 104 105, 106, 107, 110, 114, 115, 116, 117, 118, 123, 127, 138, 142, 154

fear 3, 6, 11, 59, 82, 83, 84, 85, 89, 128, 142, 151, 153
fear of rejection 83, 84, 85, 89, 153
feedback 3, 25, 27, 37, 42, 43, 44, 45, 50, 51, 52, 53, 57, 82, 83, 84, 88, 89, 99, 108, 112, 113, 114, 116, 118, 119, 126, 127, 129, 130, 137, 138, 139, 141, 143, 150, 151, 155
fire swamp 6, 7
first day 14
flame v, 65
flaws xxii, 47, 57, 58, 62, 139, 142, 143
flexibility xviii
flow 76
foundation xvii, xviii, xx, 1, 4, 27, 29, 55, 94
freedom xv, xvii, xviii, xix, 144
free write 35
further reading vi, 161

gatekeepers 139, 140, 143
goals v, ix, xv, xvi, xxi, 1, 3, 10, 11, 16, 19, 20, 21, 22, 23, 24, 25, 26, 27, 29, 65, 66, 67, 68, 73
grade anxiety 106, 107
grades 8, 58, 96, 97, 101, 103, 106, 107, 108, 110, 154
graduate career 20, 93

graduate program xxii, 13, 26, 44, 93, 94, 95, 97, 98, 101, 103, 117, 154
graduate school i, ix, xiii, xv, xvii, xxii, 3, 13, 19, 36, 42, 57, 58, 62, 66, 70, 80, 83, 91, 93, 94, 95, 96, 97, 99, 100, 101, 102, 103, 104, 105, 106, 107, 108, 109, 110, 111, 112, 114, 118, 120, 132, 147
grant money xviii, 48, 100
grant preparation 13, 15
gratitude, grateful 47, 53, 114, 127
graveyard 33, 35
GRE 93, 96, 101, 102, 154
group discussion 134
group goals xxi, 10, 19, 21, 22, 23, 24, 26, 27

heat index 43, 46
"hot potato" 29, 41–3, 45, 144

idealist 57, 58, 61, 62
ideas x, xi, xvi, xxi, 9, 11, 12, 15, 22, 24, 25, 27, 33, 34, 35, 38, 40, 43, 44, 48, 49, 51, 52, 53, 57, 58, 61, 62, 64, 66, 67, 68, 69, 71, 77, 86, 94, 99, 103, 111, 112, 114, 115, 116, 121, 136, 137, 138, 140, 150
importance x, xxi, 4, 5, 10, 11, 12, 20, 28, 38, 48, 59, 97, 121, 129, 130, 144
inferior journals 84
intellectual stimulation 65, 66, 68, 73
interests i, xviii, xix, xxii, 3, 11, 13, 14, 15, 17, 22, 24, 27, 38, 49, 51, 69, 70, 71, 75, 80, 83, 85, 93, 94, 95, 96, 98, 101, 102, 106, 115, 116, 120, 121, 122, 136, 137, 154
Internet surfing 6, 11, 69, 78
intrinsic motivation xv, xvii, xix, 128
isolation 48, 49, 121, 125

know-it-all xxi, 57, 58, 62, 63, 64

legacy xv, xvii, xix, 126
less formal presentations 26
literature reviews 13, 15, 25, 58, 64, 96, 123, 140, 142
literature updates 140

Index

location of grad school 100
loneliness 49

managing projects xx, xxi, 36, 40
manuscript 15, 16, 19, 20, 22, 23, 25, 26, 27, 28, 29, 31, 33, 34, 35, 37–47, 52, 53, 59, 60, 63, 82–9, 96, 99, 109, 115, 117, 124, 139, 140, 141, 142, 143, 144, 149, 150, 151, 157, 158
manuscript progression chart xi, 40, 41
maximize old ties 121,
mentor x, xxii, 91, 93, 97, 98, 99, 100, 101, 110, 112, 113, 114, 115, 116, 117, 118, 119, 121, 124, 126–31, 145, 155, 156, 157, 103, 106, 108, 109, 110, 116
mentoring students xxii, 110, 112, 114, 115, 117, 118, 126, 127, 128, 130, 156, 157
milestones 59, 72, 73
model xx, 29, 31, 35, 36
motivation i, xx, xxi, xxii, 1, 12, 13, 16, 19, 20, 21, 22, 23, 25, 26, 27, 29, 37, 38, 39, 40, 41, 53, 55, 65, 67, 72, 73, 77, 79, 81, 83, 103, 112, 114, 117, 128, 129, 130, 137, 149, 156
multiple lines of research 16, 114, 115, 144
multitasking 77

networking 69, 70, 80, 99, 101, 115, 116, 128, 134
"Next" 82, 86, 87, 90
numbers game 82, 87, 89

obstacles xvi, 3, 6, 11, 106
opportunity xviii, 27, 47, 48, 51, 71, 72, 88, 95, 98, 116, 117, 123, 130
outline xxi, 29, 35

pack a lunch 67, 68
paradigm shift 105, 107, 111
passion xxi, 12, 13, 14, 15, 86, 93, 128, 144, 164
passive income 47, 48, 144
perfectionist 57, 58, 59, 60, 61, 152
permissive 127, 128, 131
physical health 65, 66, 73

pitfalls x, xv, xvi, xx, xxi, 53, 55, 56, 58, 89, 91, 144
planning ahead 27, 94
post-docs 115, 118
practical help 126, 128, 129, 130
practicality 11, 13, 15
preparation 8, 13, 15, 26, 41, 63, 115, 123, 132, 133, 136, 137, 138
presentation opportunities 26
prevention v, xv, xix, xx, xxi, 55, 56, 58, 60, 62, 64, 89, 118, 144, 145
pride ix, 57, 60, 126, 130
principles ix, x, xi, xii, xvi, xvii, xix, xx, 1, 22, 29, 48, 55, 59, 65, 86, 89, 91, 101, 113, 114, 117, 118, 128, 132, 134, 137, 144, 145
priorities xv, xvi, xix, xx, 1, 3, 4, 6, 8, 10, 12, 45, 55, 89, 91, 110, 118, 144, 145
procrastinate, procrastinator 25, 45, 57, 59, 60, 63, 89, 105, 151
productivity i, x, xv, xvi, xix, xx, xxi, xxii, 1, 4, 6, 11, 13, 16, 20, 28, 29, 31, 46, 47, 49, 53, 55, 57, 58, 59, 65, 66, 68, 69, 70, 73, 77, 78, 80, 81, 83, 84, 97, 98, 108, 116, 117, 118, 121, 122, 127, 129, 130, 134, 135, 136, 139, 140, 141, 143, 144, 145, 147, 156, 161, 163
professional mentality 91, 103, 105, 106, 107, 108, 109, 110, 111, 112, 118, 145
programmatic research 13, 15, 16, 38
promotions i, xv, 110, 127, 141, 144
proofreading 117, 124
publication lag time 39, 43
purpose xii, xxiii, 9, 21, 22, 26, 31, 32, 34, 38, 57, 63, 104, 106, 112

quality of journals 49, 98

raises xv, xvii, xviii, xix, 4, 127, 144
read to write 31, 32, 33, 35
recognition 13, 15
recruit 116, 117
reducing preparation time 133
reference sections 15, 124
refining your skills 140
reinvent the wheel 133

168   Index

rejection xxi, 3, 7, 20, 31, 37, 38, 39, 40, 41, 42, 43, 44, 45, 47, 50, 53, 56, 82, 83, 84, 85, 86, 87, 88, 89, 145, 151, 153, 154
research goals 10, 19, 21, 22, 23, 24, 26, 27
research prioritizer 8, 9
respect 43, 44, 49, 72, 84, 95, 120, 129, 144
reviewing articles 63, 139, 140, 141
revise and resubmit 20, 38, 42, 44, 45, 150
rule of three 37, 40, 41, 141

saving time 67, 134
schedule 10, 43, 44, 59, 67, 81, 106, 110, 123, 132, 134, 136, 137
seeking mentorship 112, 114, 119
selecting a topic of study 13, 14, 94
selective 49, 122
self-assessment i, xi, 145, 147
self-introspection ix, 65, 69, 74
service 22, 70, 88, 143
set yourself apart 95, 96
"sharpening the saw" 66
simplified writing 31, 32, 33, 35
skills xvii, xxi, 27, 49, 50, 76, 114, 117, 123, 140, 151
sleep 48, 65, 68
slow coauthors 38
snow fort principle 37, 38
social interaction 65, 66, 69, 70, 73, 74, 136
social media 78, 153
spread your wings 100, 101
stages 9, 21, 41, 60, 70, 89, 91, 96, 99, 109, 120, 130, 144, 145
statistical skills 49, 50
staying busy 37, 39, 40
strategies 7, 10, 11, 12, 15, 21, 31, 32, 33, 35, 36, 39, 40, 44, 46, 48, 56, 59, 63, 64, 65, 79, 80, 81, 85, 88, 89, 91, 96, 110, 118, 128, 135, 137, 138, 140, 144, 145
strengths 27, 50, 77, 80, 85, 96, 99, 144
student attendance 132, 134, 135, 137, 138
student emails 80, 134
student mentality 91, 103, 105, 108, 109, 110, 145

students 3, 7, 22, 26, 27, 37, 42, 43, 47, 50, 51, 57, 59, 60, 62, 64, 67, 70, 75, 80, 81, 84, 91, 93, 95, 97, 98, 99, 100, 101, 102, 103, 104, 108, 109, 110, 112, 113, 114, 115, 117, 118, 120, 121, 122, 123, 124, 126, 127, 128, 129, 130, 131, 132, 133, 135, 136, 137, 138, 144, 145
study 96
style 31, 32, 33, 35, 50, 64, 66, 80, 99, 115, 128, 131, 134
submission of manuscripts 10, 19, 23, 27, 43, 44, 82, 83, 84, 89
success 3, 7, 10, 13, 14, 15, 19, 23, 39, 40, 44, 45, 46, 47, 49, 59, 65, 66, 73, 82, 83, 85, 86, 87, 88, 89, 94, 96, 101, 105, 108, 110, 113, 114, 115, 116, 121, 122, 124, 126, 128, 130, 132, 145
sustained engagement 38
synergy 48, 117, 121

taking action 443
talents 70, 76, 97
teaching 5, 7, 8, 9, 11, 21, 80, 97, 99, 100, 104, 112, 113, 120, 123, 126, 128, 129, 130, 132, 133, 134, 136, 137, 138, 141, 145, 147, 157
teaching assistants 3, 130, 132, 134, 136, 138, 157
teamwork 22, 144
technology distractions 75, 78, 79, 81
tenure 4, 5, 42, 65, 66, 97, 98, 99, 105, 110, 129, 130, 140, 141, 144
test 25, 39, 40, 63, 85, 89, 96, 107, 110, 122
texting 76, 78, 79
time 1, 3, 4, 5, 8, 9, 10, 11, 12, 14, 15, 16, 20, 21, 22, 26, 27, 29, 31, 32, 34, 35, 36, 37, 39, 40, 41, 42, 43, 44, 45, 48, 49, 52, 54, 57, 58, 59, 60, 61, 62, 63, 64, 65, 66, 67, 68, 69, 70, 71, 72, 73, 75, 76, 77, 79, 80, 81, 83, 84, 87, 88, 89, 95, 96, 99, 100, 103, 104, 105, 106, 107, 108, 109, 110, 114, 115, 116, 117, 118, 121, 122, 123, 124, 125, 126, 129, 130, 131, 132, 133, 134, 135, 136, 137, 138, 139, 140, 141, 142, 143, 144, 145; management of 9, 19, 37, 76, 137; preparation time 8, 13, 15, 26, 41, 63, 115, 123, 132, 133, 136, 137, 138; wasting of 49, 115,

time diary 4, 12, 81
track record 3, 49, 93, 97, 101, 115, 116
transitions 105, 106, 120, 124, 145

undergraduate breaks 103, 108, 110
undergraduates 14, 37, 51, 68, 82, 86, 93, 94, 95, 96, 99, 100, 101, 102, 104, 105, 106, 107, 108, 110, 117, 123, 126, 136, 145
university milestones 103, 106, 108, 110, 116
university resources 51, 67, 71
updates 47, 53, 75, 79, 140
urgency quadrants 4

validation 65, 71, 72, 73, 137
value 3, 27, 35, 43, 44, 50, 53, 66, 116, 122, 127, 129, 141, 142
vision 19, 20
volunteering 25, 27, 69, 70

weaknesses 50, 147
working for pay 109
working for your future 109
workload 47, 48, 84
writing an introduction 15, 31, 32, 33, 35, 36, 63
writing process 29, 31, 32, 33, 35, 145
writing style 31, 32, 33, 35